A Physician's Insights on the Great Physician

Keys to Experiencing God's Healing Power

by Bayless Conley

Answers Press
© 2025 by Bayless Conley
First Printing 2025

Answers with Bayless Conley
PO Box 417
Los Alamitos, CA 90720

Visit our website at www.BaylessConley.tv.

ISBN: 978-1-953297-11-2
eBook: 978-1-953297-40-2
Hardcover: 978-1-953297-39-6

All Scripture quotations, unless otherwise indicated, are taken from the New King James Version®, Copyright © 1982 by Thomas Nelson. Used by permission. All rights reserved.

Scripture quotations marked AMPC are taken from the Amplified® Bible (Classic Edition), Copyright © 1954, 1958, 1962, 1964, 1965, 1987 by The Lockman Foundation. Used by permission. All rights reserved.

Scripture quotations marked ERV are taken from the Holy Bible: Easy-to-Read Version®, Copyright © 2014 by Bible League International. Used by permission.

Scripture quotations marked KJV are taken from The Holy Bible, King James Version, public domain.

Scripture quotations marked MSG are taken from The Message, Copyright © 1993, 2002, 2018 by Eugene H. Peterson. Used by permission of NavPress. All rights reserved. Represented by Tyndale House Publishers.

Scripture quotations marked NLT are taken from the Holy Bible, New Living Translation, Copyright © 1996, 2004, 2015 by Tyndale House Foundation. Used by permission of Tyndale House Publishers, Inc., Carol Stream, Illinois 60188. All rights reserved.

Scripture quotations marked WNT are taken from the Weymouth New Testament, also known as *The New Testament in Modern Speech*, public domain.

All rights reserved. No part of this publication may be reproduced, stored in a retrieval system, or transmitted in any form or by any means—electronic, mechanical, photocopying, recording, or otherwise—without prior written permission from the author.

Printed in the United States of America

Contents

Preface 5

PART ONE – THE GOSPEL OF LUKE

01	Filled with the Spirit	11
02	Lessons from a Leper	27
03	The Power of the Lord Was Present	41
04	A Miracle in the Synagogue	53
05	Great Faith	63
06	A Funeral Interrupted	73
07	Healed of Evil Spirits and Infirmities	83
08	Twelve Years of Sunshine and Twelve Years of Suffering	97
09	Called, Given, and Sent	109
10	Bound by Satan, Freed by Christ	125
11	Healing on the Sabbath . . . Again	137
12	Mercy, Mercy, and More Mercy	151

PART TWO – THE BOOK OF ACTS

13	The Lord's Continued Ministry Through His Church	159
14	Captivated by the Supernatural	165
15	Resistance from the Sadducees	177
16	Points to Ponder	193
17	Miracles, Martyrs, and More Miracles	207
18	Aeneas and Dorcas	227
19	Sent Out by the Holy Spirit	239
20	A Spirit of Divination and Unusual Miracles	253
21	Dead Men, Shipwrecks, and Snake Bites	261
Notes	....	282
Quick Reference	....	284

Preface

Why Have We Never Been Told About This?!

Many years ago, I was invited to be a guest speaker at a local Bible study. It was held in the home of an acquaintance of mine, and though I had never met most of those in attendance, they all knew one another well. The same group of people had been meeting together on a weekly basis for some time.

That evening, I shared on the subject of healing, and it was obvious to me that a couple of those in attendance, though polite, were not comfortable with the subject. After laying out a scriptural case for healing with the group, I asked if any had need of prayer. One gentleman spoke up, stating that he had severe back problems and was at that moment in quite a lot of pain.

What happened next is something I never shall forget. I laid my hands on him and prayed a simple prayer of healing for his back. After the prayer, he stood with an astonished look on his face. "All of the pain is gone! I'm healed!" he exclaimed. He began to bend and touch his toes, saying over and over, "The pain is gone! I'm healed."

One of those present who had looked decidedly uncomfortable said, "How can this be?" It turns out that he was a medical doctor and was skeptical of divine healing. He examined the man now claiming to be healed. They were friends, and the doctor was well acquainted with his condition. "But how?" the doctor asked again.

From his cursory examination and the fact that his friend was emphatically exclaiming that all the pain was suddenly gone, and it being obvious that his full mobility had suddenly been restored, the doctor agreed that he had indeed been healed somehow.

He then turned to me and said, "Please explain this." I went over some of the same verses on healing that I had taught on that night and spent quite a while citing other healing promises in the Bible. I talked about how much of Jesus' earthly ministry revolved around healing the sick and that He hasn't changed. I also pointed out a number of passages that spoke of healing as a part of Christ's redemptive work. When I finished, the doctor was angry—not at me, but at the fact that he had never been shown these things before.

This doctor was a solid believer who genuinely loved the Lord, and he had attended church regularly for many years. He said, "I've been going to church a long time. What I want to know is, why have we never been told about this before?! To that question, I didn't have an answer.

It was a remarkable evening. To witness the Lord heal someone in such an astounding and sudden manner and to watch the eyes of that physician open to the biblical truth of divine healing was marvelous. He had dedicated his life to helping people recover from sickness and injury through natural means, and now to realize that his Savior was still in the healing business had to have been mind-blowing for him. In this book, we are going to look at the writings of another physician, one who was intimately acquainted with divine healing. The Bible calls him "Luke the beloved physician" (Colossians 4:14). He wrote the gospel that bears his name as well as the book of Acts. He was a physician by training who accompanied the apostle Paul during some of his missionary endeavors. Due to his medical training, no doubt, he observes and comments on the healing ministry of Jesus in his Gospel, as well as the healing ministry carried out by the Holy Spirit through the Church, as recorded in Acts, with a certain amount of detail, which, in some cases, is not used by the other gospel writers.

As you journey forward in this book, I want to encourage you to read it prayerfully. Take your time, and as often as you can, read the Bible stories that I quote from and refer to in their entirety. Read with an open heart and trust the Holy Spirit to help you understand and apply Dr. Luke's insights on the Great Physician.

Part One

THE GOSPEL OF LUKE

Dr. Luke's account of the earthly life and ministry of the Lord Jesus is full of wonderful examples of people who were the recipients of the Master's healing touch.

Their stories are varied, as were the methods that Jesus used to bring healing and restoration to them. As we examine each case of healing along with the events that surround them, I believe that your faith will come alive.

My prayer is that just like the people in Luke's Gospel you will come to know Jesus as your Healer as well.

CHAPTER

1

Filled with the Spirit

As we begin reading in Luke's Gospel, we find that Jesus' ministry began after He was filled with the Spirit. In fact, we are told that *the Holy Spirit descended* on Jesus (Luke 3:22), Jesus was *filled with and led by the Spirit* (Luke 4:1), and after His temptation in the wilderness, He returned to Galilee in **the power of the Spirit** (Luke 4:14–15).

Jesus began His ministry at the age of 30 (Luke 3:23). Prior to that, He did not perform miracles, heal the sick, or cast out any demons. He was just as much the Son of God at age 5, 15, 20, 25, and 29 as He was at age 30. What made the difference? Though there may possibly be some secondary reasons, the one major difference revealed to us is that He was filled with and empowered by the Holy Spirit at age 30.

Though Jesus was the Son of God, He did not minister as the Son of God in the sense that He brought some cosmic, heavenly powers with Him to earth. In the book of Philippians, it is declared of Jesus that,

> ⁶Who, although being essentially one with God and in the form of God [possessing the fullness of the attributes which make God God], did not think this equality with God was a thing to be eagerly grasped or retained, ⁷but stripped Himself [of all privileges and rightful dignity], so as to assume the guise of a servant (slave), in that He became like men and was born a human being. (Philippians 2:6–7 AMPC)

Jesus ministered as a man filled with, led by, and empowered by the Holy Spirit. And if Jesus, the sinless Son of God, yet functioning as the perfect man, needed to be filled with, led by, and empowered by the Spirit, how much more are we in need of the Holy Spirit's vital ministry?

He Reads from Isaiah About Himself

Immediately upon returning to Galilee, Jesus entered into public ministry, going throughout the region teaching in all their synagogues. When He came to Nazareth, where He had been brought up, He went into the synagogue on the Sabbath and stood up to read. Once He was handed the scroll of Isaiah, He looked up the specific place where it was written about Him and His ministry:

> ¹⁸"The Spirit of the Lord is upon Me, because He has anointed Me to preach the gospel to the poor; He has sent Me to heal the brokenhearted, to proclaim liberty to the captives and recovery of sight to the blind, to set at liberty those who are oppressed; ¹⁹to proclaim the acceptable year of the Lord." (Luke 4:18–19)

When He had finished reading, He sat down and told everyone, "Today this Scripture is fulfilled" (Luke 4:14–21; Isaiah 61:1–2).

In doing this, Jesus was basically saying that the Spirit was upon Him and had anointed Him to minister to five kinds of people: the ***poor***, the ***brokenhearted***, those in ***captivity***, the ***blind***, and the ***oppressed***. What a description of humanity! What a description of our own generation! In the Scriptures, at least three of these five descriptions are applied to sickness or physical conditions: *captivity* (when Job was healed and delivered, it was expressed by saying the Lord turned his *captivity* in Job 42:10 KJV), *blind*, and *oppressed* (God referred to the sick that were healed by Christ as having been previously *oppressed* by the devil in Acts 10:38).

The Acceptable Year of the Lord

Jesus finished His reading from Isaiah by saying that He had been anointed to proclaim "the acceptable year of the Lord" (v. 19). The acceptable year of the Lord is one of the terms used to describe the Year of Jubilee (Leviticus 25). The Year of Jubilee occurred once every fifty years in Israel. It occurred at the time of Passover, but it was unique from any other Passover celebration. On the Year of Jubilee, the Passover lamb was slain, a trumpet was sounded, and every man was then free to return to his possessions.

This means that, if you had lost your ancestral home, it was returned at Jubilee. If you had become poor and sold yourself into indentured servitude out of necessity, you were set free on Jubilee. Whatever you had lost was recovered on that fiftieth year. It was a great kindness instituted by God for His people who had come on hard times and lost what was previously theirs, but it was also more. It was a type and a shadow pointing to Christ where it found its ultimate fulfillment.

Through the fall of man in the garden, humanity had become destitute and poor spiritually. We had become brokenhearted, captive, blind, and oppressed! But Jesus came to change all of that. He is our Jubilee!

Because of His redemptive work, and through the power of the Holy Spirit, we can return to our possessions!

We can have a rich, meaningful relationship with God, our needs can be met, our broken hearts can be healed, we can be freed from spiritual captivity, mental captivity, and the captivity of sickness. The blind can be healed, and we can be liberated from oppression in spirit, soul, and body. The Amplified Bible, Classic Edition renders this word *oppressed* as "downtrodden, bruised, crushed, and broken down by calamity."

If that describes you, there is good news. Jesus came so that we could return to our lost possessions of life, peace, blessing, and health.

Today Faith

Eric was four years old and loved the beach. The only problem was that his family lived a hundred miles inland. His first time at the beach was one summer on a family vacation, and he just couldn't get enough of it. They had rented a small cottage on the sand, and Eric had spent nearly every moment digging around on the shore, catching little crabs, and wading in the warm, shallow, gulf water.

One evening after the family returned home from their memorable trip, Eric said, "Dad, can we please go back to the beach?" "Sure, Eric," his dad said distractedly. Eric disappeared and in about ten minutes reappeared in the kitchen wearing his swimsuit and carrying his beach pail and a small shovel. "What are you doing, son?" His dad asked him with a grin. "You said we were going to the beach!" "We will, Eric," his father responded. "Just not today."

After Jesus read the beautiful promise of restoration and healing foretold by the acceptable year of the Lord (or Year of Jubilee), He didn't say it would be available someday. He said it was fulfilled today! Restoration and healing are available to you now—today.

When Jesus came to the tomb of Lazarus in John 11, Martha said, "If You had been here my brother would not have died" (v. 21). Jesus told her, "Your brother will rise again" (v. 23). To which she responded, "I know that he will rise again in the resurrection at the last day" (v. 24). Jesus, however, raised Lazarus that very day! Martha is like so many. They have faith for the past and faith for the future but no faith for right now. The Lord is looking for today faith. Do you believe that Jesus is our Jubilee? Do you believe that He can work on your behalf today?

Sometimes Those Who Have the Greatest Access to Healing and Blessing Experience It the Least

The Lord's interaction with those in His home synagogue is not finished yet. After Jesus declared the fulfillment of the Jubilee to the people, Luke tells us,

> ²²So all bore witness to Him, and marveled at the gracious words which proceeded out of His mouth. And they said, "Is this not Joseph's son?" ²³He said to them, "You will surely say this proverb to Me, 'Physician, heal yourself! Whatever we have heard done in Capernaum, do also here in Your country.'" (Luke 4:22–23)

He was prophesying to them. The day will come when these same people will say, "What we've heard about you doing in other towns, do here in your hometown." Interestingly enough, sometimes those who have the greatest access to healing and blessing experience it the least. It all has to do with attitude and response, as we shall see by what Jesus shares next:

> ²⁴Then He said, "Assuredly, I say to you, no prophet is accepted in his own country. ²⁵But I tell you truly, many widows were in Israel in the days of Elijah, when the heaven

was shut up three years and six months, and there was a great famine throughout all the land; ²⁶but to none of them was Elijah sent except to Zarephath, in the region of Sidon, to a woman who was a widow. ²⁷And many lepers were in Israel in the time of Elisha the prophet, and none of them was cleansed except Naaman the Syrian." (Luke 4:24–27)

The people from His hometown of Nazareth did not accept Jesus. They came up with reasons not to believe in Him or in what He said. Their attitude and response to Him blocked any blessing that might have come their way.

Foreigners Got the Blessing

Jesus then went on to share two stories that everyone in that synagogue would have known by heart. The widow of Zarephath and Naaman the Syrian. The widow would have come under the *poor* category of those whom Jesus was sent to. She had her needs supernaturally met by God. Naaman would have been under the *captive* or *oppressed* category, as he was sick with leprosy. He was supernaturally healed by God. They were both foreigners and they received the blessing while those in Israel went without!

Why was the widow's need met during the famine, and why was Naaman cleansed of leprosy and not others in Israel who had a right to those blessings by covenant? We need only to look at the record of their stories to see why, although Jesus summarized it when He said that His ministry would not be accepted in His own country (vv. 23–24). God is not moved merely by need. It is faith and a receptive heart that bring His power to bear in the circumstances of life.

The Widow

The widow of Zarephath obeyed the word of the Lord at Elijah's mouth even though it made no sense, naturally speaking. There was a severe famine in the land, and she and her son were on the verge of death. Elijah promised her that if she would make him a cake first from her meager resources, her bin of flour and jar of oil would be supernaturally replenished.

She didn't come up with reasons not to believe him, like those in Nazareth had done with Jesus. Instead, she accepted and acted upon the promise as soon as it was given, and a sustained miracle occurred. Her and her son's needs were amply supplied until the drought and famine had ended (1 Kings 17:8–16).

Naaman the Syrian

Naaman was brave, wealthy, respected, and famous in his native land of Syria, but he became sick with leprosy. Sickness is no respecter of persons. It visits rich and poor, strong and weak, famous and unknown, male and female, all races, classes, and cultures.

A young Israelite girl who served Naaman's wife told her there was a prophet in Israel that God was using to bring healing. When Naaman heard that news, he latched on to it tightly and believed. He didn't come up with reasons not to believe. He was hopeful and aggressively went after an answer.

Here are a few excuses that Naaman could have easily come up with if he chose to do so. He could have said:

- "What does a little slave girl know about anything anyway? Why should I take her word for it?"

- "I've been leading raids against Israel. Even if it were true, no one from Israel would help me."

- "Even if it is true, I would probably never find the prophet."
- "His healing ministry probably isn't for everyone. I bet it's just for Israelites, not Syrians like me."
- "If it were really true, I would have heard about it before this. It's probably just a fanciful rumor."

Naaman didn't say anything like that. He believed in supernatural healing and he went into Israel to seek out the prophet with his king's blessing. Once he found Elisha, he was given instructions that didn't make any more sense than those given by Elijah to the widow at Zarephath. But once he acted upon them (dipping in the Jordan River seven times) he was cured of his leprosy (2 Kings 5:1–14).

Both the widow and this Syrian general believed and acted upon a promise from God at the mouths of His servants. Rather than looking for reasons not to believe, they were open, receptive, and obedient. Our attitude and response to the Lord and His promises have everything to do with us experiencing the blessings that He has so graciously provided.

Purchased at Calvary

Freedom, liberty, peace, and healing have been purchased for us at Calvary. Jesus is our Jubilee. We have a blood-bought right to return to our possessions. I am sounding the gospel, Jubilee trumpet! The time of freedom is upon us. The acceptable year of the Lord has come! But as we all know, the fact that someone has become a Christian does not make all of the provisions of redemption automatic.

We need to go after those promised blessings like Naaman. We need to believe and act upon the promises like the widow at Zarephath. We cannot sit complacently by and expect those blessings to just fall on us out of the sky. We need to accept the gospel we hear preached—all of it. God is looking for those who will accept, believe, and act upon His promises of peace, healing, guidance, and strength, just like they believe and accept His promises of forgiveness.

The Contrast of Faith

I once heard a pastor share a story that, in my opinion, really showed the contrast between a lazy, unbelieving heart and a faith-filled, receptive heart. He had heard through the grapevine that one of his members was sick. It surprised him that neither the sick man nor his family had directly contacted him, as the church was not large and he often taught on the subjects of prayer and healing. He had supposed that as soon as the man had become sick they would have sought prayer from the pastor or elders.

He contacted the family and arranged for a time to come by to pray for his sick parishioner. When he got to the house he went up to the front door and knocked. No response. He knocked again. No response. He began banging on the door and eventually the wife answered it. "Oh, it's you," she said. "He's in the back room, but I think you're wasting your time." Then she walked off, leaving him to find her husband on his own.

When he finally found the correct room, he went in and greeted the man and offered to pray for him and anoint him with the small bottle of oil he had brought with him. "If you want to," the man said in a disinterested tone. The pastor prayed, anointed the man, and left with the distinct impression that he had not been welcome in their home. The prayer bore no fruit.

I'm Not a Christian

A few days later, the pastor received a phone call at the church. It was from a mother whose children were sick. "Hello," she said. "I was calling to see if your church anointed the sick with oil and prayed for healing." "Yes, we do," the pastor said. "Wonderful!" she exclaimed. "My children are sick and I need someone to pray for them. I don't go to church though. Will you still come?" "Of course," the pastor responded. He got her address and said, "I'll be right over."

When he drove up, she was waiting for him on the curb. "Thank you for coming," she said. "Now I told you that I don't go to church, and the truth is I'm not a Christian. But I was reading in the Bible in the book of James that the sick could call for the elders of the church, and if the elders would put oil on the sick . . . you brought your oil, didn't you? Good. Anyway, if they would put oil on them and pray, the Lord would heal them. I may not attend church, but I do believe the Bible, and I know God loves my kids. I believe if you pray they will be healed."

She ushered him into the kids' room, announcing to the kids what was going to happen. The pastor said the atmosphere was so thick with faith that to him it almost seemed tangible. He prayed and her children were healed.

Just like with the widow and Naaman, it was someone outside of the covenant who got the blessing because of their attitude and response to the promise.

I Don't Like That

It is true. A non-Christian may get healed or blessed while the child of God goes without, depending on their heart attitude and actions in connection with the promises. I realize that there will be some who think or say, "I don't like that!" Another truth is that such people fit right in with the narrative in Luke 4. Look at what happens when Jesus tells the Jews in the synagogue about the foreigners who were healed and blessed while God's people went without.

²⁸So all those in the synagogue, when they heard these things, were filled with wrath, ²⁹and rose up and thrust Him out of the city; and they led Him to the brow of the hill on which their city was built, that they might throw Him down over the cliff. ³⁰Then passing through the midst of them, He went His way. (Luke 4:28–30)

Looking for Other Hungry Hearts

Jesus, having passed through the crowd, went His way. *His way* then, as it is today, was to look for hungry hearts that would embrace the message He came to bring.

³¹Then He went down to Capernaum, a city of Galilee, and was teaching them on the Sabbaths. ³²And they were astonished at His teaching, for His word was with authority. ³³Now in the synagogue there was a man who had a spirit of an unclean demon. And he cried out with a loud voice, ³⁴saying, "Let us alone! What have we to do with You, Jesus of Nazareth? Did You come to destroy us? I know who You are—the Holy One of God!"

³⁵But Jesus rebuked him, saying, "Be quiet, and come out of him!" And when the demon had thrown him in their midst, it came out of him and did not hurt him. ³⁶Then they were all amazed and spoke among themselves, saying, "What a word this is! For with authority and power He commands the unclean spirits, and they come out." ³⁷And the report about Him went out into every place in the surrounding region. (Luke 4:31–37)

Basically, Jesus has gone out to do exactly what was proclaimed of Him in verses 18–19. He is preaching and setting the captives free! It is interesting to note that the man with the unclean demon possessing him was with the worshipers in the synagogue. Satan attends church as well as the tombs (Luke 8:27), but Jesus has power over demons wherever they may be.

When Jesus cast the unclean demon out of the man, He was forceful about doing so. Jesus rebuked the demon and said, "Be quiet (literally, "be muzzled"), and come out of him!" In fact, the Greek word translated *rebuked* (v. 35) is a very harsh word.

Jesus' tone was not mild when He addressed the demon. He was all business. He commanded. He did not carry on a conversation. The people recognized the authority of His teaching (v. 32) and the authority and power He had and exercised over demons (v. 36). Both arenas of authority astonished them.

No Ordinary Doctor

As we continue following the healing ministry of Jesus in Luke 4, Dr. Luke begins using some of the medical terms of his day to describe what takes place. But as he does so, he also makes it clear that Jesus was no ordinary doctor.

> [38]Now He arose from the synagogue and entered Simon's house. But Simon's wife's mother was sick with a high fever, and they made request of Him concerning her. [39]So He stood over her and rebuked the fever, and it left her. And immediately she arose and served them. (Luke 4:38–39)

In those times, fevers were divided into two categories: *great (or high) fevers* and *little fevers*. Dr. Luke, in telling about the healing of Simon's mother-in-law, uses a medical term informing us that she had a great fever.[1] This was not a fever associated with a cold or the flu, but something virulent, dangerous, and even life-threatening.

Another medical term is used to describe the posture that Jesus took with this woman who was so seriously sick. He stood over her, which in medical terms of the day describes a doctor visiting and tending to a patient.[2] But Jesus did something no ordinary doctor of the day would have done—He rebuked the fever!

He used the same harsh Greek word to drive out sickness that He used to drive out demons (vv. 35, 39). Jesus did not treat sickness as a friend. He dealt with it in the same way He dealt with evil spirits!

It is also noteworthy that they (probably referring to Simon and his wife) made a request for Jesus to heal her. They didn't just assume that if it was His will, He would do so. James tells us that "you do not have because you do not ask" (James 4:2).

Once the mother-in-law was healed, she immediately began to serve the Lord and those who were present. No less than six times did God say to Pharaoh, "Let my people go *that they may serve me*" (Exodus 7–10). Our main motivation for desiring healing should be to better serve the Lord. Our hearts and bodies should be dedicated to Him and to His service.

All, Any, and Every One

Some will say, "But healing isn't available to everyone. Jesus only healed a select few." Dr. Luke would disagree with that. The next thing we read is:

> [40]When the sun was setting, ***all those who had any that were sick with various diseases brought them to Him; and He laid His hands on every one of them and healed them***. [41]And demons also came out of many, crying out and saying, "You are the Christ, the Son of God!" And He,

rebuking them, did not allow them to speak, for they knew that He was the Christ. (Luke 4:40–41, emphasis mine)

When it came to healing those in Capernaum, Luke tells us that **all** those who had **any** sick brought them to Jesus and He laid hands on **every one** of them and healed them. "Jesus Christ is the same yesterday, today, and forever" (Hebrews 13:8).

For anyone reading this now, I would encourage you to immediately dismiss the notion that healing may not be for you. If it is for one, it is for all. If it is part of Christ's redemptive work, it is for all (Romans 10:12; Isaiah 53:4–5; Matthew 8:16–17; 1 Peter 2:24).

A Rumor and a Roar

A crowd of people from Capernaum wanted Him to stay, but Jesus left them, knowing that He had to preach in other cities also. And so He went, bringing the good news to the *poor, brokenhearted, captive, blind,* and *oppressed* throughout the synagogues of Galilee (Luke 4:42–44).

In Luke 4:14, it says that "news of Him went out through all the surrounding region." The Greek word translated as "news" is *pheme*, which more precisely means "rumor" or "bits of a story here and there."

Luke 4:37 says that "the report of Him went out into every place." The Greek word translated "report" is *echos*, which could be translated as "roar." The rumor turned into a roar! Everyone was talking about Him. There was a stir everywhere. But it means "a confused stir."

By the time we get to Luke 5:15, we are told that "the report went around concerning Him all the more, and great multitudes came together to hear and to be healed by Him of their infirmities." The Greek word translated as "report" in this verse is *logos*. It is translated many times in the New Testament as "word" and implies "an intelligent apprehension."

People began to understand His message. It went through the stages of *rumor* to *roar* (where the whole region was moved) to finally becoming a *word*—"a clear, distinct message."[3]

The result was that multitudes came together to hear and to be healed by Him of their infirmities.

Where are you when it comes to this Jubilee message of healing and liberty? Is it still a rumor where you just have bits and pieces and you are hoping that it is true? Or is it more of a roar where you find yourself swept up with the buzz and the excitement of things? Or has it become a clear and distinct word where there is no confusion about the message?

The multitudes in Luke 5:15 came to Jesus with a specific purpose. They came to hear and be healed because they had understood a clear message. If you are truly hungry to understand more about our Savior's ongoing ministry of healing, and if you want to experience the liberty and freedom that He has brought to us through His redemptive work on the cross, please read on.

CHAPTER

2

Lessons from a Leper

¹²And it happened when He was in a certain city, that behold, a man who was full of leprosy saw Jesus; and he fell on his face and implored Him, saying, "Lord, if You are willing, You can make me clean." ¹³Then He put out His hand and touched him, saying, "I am willing; be cleansed." Immediately the leprosy left him. (Luke 5:12–13)

When Luke tells the story of the leper that came to Jesus, he again uses a medical term to describe things. He said the man was *full* of leprosy, a detail that is left out by the other gospel writers when they relay the story. Medically speaking, when Dr. Luke states that the man was full of leprosy, it meant that it had affected his entire body and was at its worst and most terrible stage. This poor man was not only considered *untouchable*, but as far as human means were concerned he was *incurable*. He was beyond human help.

Focus

We were hiking up a small creek in the San Bernardino mountains. I had taken our oldest son, Harrison, out of school for the day to do some trout fishing together. We were catching a few native trout here and there as we continued hiking up the canyon. Eventually we came to a large waterfall that cascaded into a deep, crystal-clear pool loaded with fish.

We fished to our hearts' content and then decided to go up higher to see what other treasures this little creek would produce. We soon found that this waterfall seemed to be the end of the trail. There was no way around on either side. I had Harrison wait while I attempted to scale the cliff next to the waterfall. It took me a while, but I made it. The only problem was that there was no way that Harrison, with his short, 11-year-old legs, could make it up the same cliff.

As I considered our dilemma, I noticed a strong rope coiled up a few feet away. It was obvious that we were not the first ones to fish the upper reaches of this little creek. After securing the rope at my end, I tossed the other end to Harrison and told him to grab it just above a knot that I had tied. "I don't think I can do this Dad," he said. "What if I fall?"

"I'll swing you out over the water and pull you up. If you fall, all's you'll get is wet," I responded.

"I don't know Dad. I'm not sure I can."

"Just trust me," I said. "Grab the rope and just keep your eyes on me and I'll do the rest."

He did it and I gently swung him out over the water. He was nervous, but I told him, "Just focus on me." I hauled him up the fifteen feet to the top and off we happily went in search of more fish.

The Scripture said that the leper **_saw Jesus_**. First and foremost, if you want to be healed, **_you need to see Jesus_**. In order to see Jesus, this man had to look away from his condition, take his eyes off of his decaying flesh, and look up to gaze upon the One who was his answer.

Receiving healing has everything to do with what we put our eyes and our focus upon. We must see Jesus!

The dying Israelites had to behold the serpent upon the pole in order to be healed. In fact, the Amplified Bible, Classic Edition, in bringing out the full meaning of the Hebrew, states that it was the ones that looked at the serpent of bronze **_attentively, expectantly, and with a steady and absorbing gaze_** that were healed (Numbers 21:8–9). Jesus Himself told us that the serpent of bronze was a type that pointed to Him and His sacrifice on the cross. He said, "And as Moses lifted up the serpent in the wilderness, even so must the Son of Man be lifted up" (John 3:14).

The Israelites could not remain occupied with the serpents slithering among them or with their snake bites and live. They had to put their attention on the answer that was hanging on the pole. If we are to be healed, we must put our attention on our answer, Jesus, who willingly hung on a cross for us.

Forty-Nine Times in Twelve Verses!

Isaiah 53 has been referred to as the great redemptive chapter of the Old Testament. In great detail it describes what Christ would go through and what He would accomplish for us through His sacrifice. Very clearly it declares that _surely He has borne our sicknesses and carried our pains and that by His stripes we are healed._

The whole chapter prophetically tells us about the full scope of what Christ would accomplish. Peace, healing, and liberation from the tyranny of sin are all spoken of as aspects of our redemption. One of the amazing things about that chapter is that Jesus is referred to no less than forty-nine times in twelve verses! You will find the pronouns "*He*," "*Him*," and "*His*" (referring to Jesus) from beginning to end. The key to that great chapter on healing is to see Jesus!

Difficult circumstances, storms, symptoms, and troubles all cry out for our attention. In no way should we ignore them, but we must be more occupied with the One who brings us through our storms and troubles. When Peter took his eyes off Jesus, he began to sink beneath the waves. He was in the middle of a miracle (walking on the water!), but when he took his focus off of Jesus and put it on the wind and waves, down he went (Matthew 14:29–31).

Posture and Petition

After considering this leper's *focus*, the next things we need to look at are his *posture* and his *petition*. Some don't receive healing because their posture isn't right, while others don't receive because they fail to petition.

The leper's posture was one of humility. "God resists the proud but gives grace to the humble" (Proverbs 3:4; James 4:6; 1 Peter 5:5). The leper fell on his face. It was a physical reflection of an inward posture of the heart. He came to Jesus with a heart of humility, submission, and reverence. We must learn to do the same.

He didn't shake his fist at Jesus and shout, "Why?! You are God's representative. Tell me why this has happened to me! It's not fair! Do you know how much I've suffered? I've been separated from family and friends. I can't work. I'm an outcast. And the constant pain! I used to be handsome, but look at me now! Why, why, why?! I'm bitter at God and at society and I have every right to be!"

No. He brought no accusations. He hurled no insults. He humbly bowed and called Jesus Lord.

Next, we see his petition. It says that he *implored* Jesus. This was not some half-hearted, casual request. He put his whole being into his request. "Lord, if You are willing, You can" (Luke 5:12). He knew that Jesus was able to heal him, but he was unsure regarding His will in the matter.

Jesus quickly cleared that up by saying, "I am willing," while at the same time reaching out His hand to touch the man. That would have been the first touch he had felt in a long time, and what a touch it was! Immediately the leprosy left him. It didn't just stop its forward progress; it left him completely!

Jesus is still the master over disease, but if we are going to be the recipients of this blessing, like the leper, we need to first clear up the Lord's willingness in the matter. Faith is based both upon trusting in the Lord's ability and knowing His will. First John 5:14–15 declares,

> [14]Now this is the confidence we have in Him, that if we ask anything according to His will, He hears us. [15]And if we know that He hears us, whatever we ask, we know that we have the petitions that we have asked of Him.

We need to hear Him saying to our hearts, "I am willing." Jesus has not changed. Walk with Him through the pages of Luke's Gospel as well as through the other three Gospels. Watch Him heal the multitudes. Consider deeply that there is no record in any of the Gospels of Jesus turning anyone away who came to Him for healing.

Jesus is the will of God in action. To see Him is to see the Father. To hear Him is to hear the Father (John 14:9; Colossians 1:15). It was only the religious leaders who came to scrutinize and condemn Him who never experienced the healing power that was available to them (Luke 5:17).

Ability and Willingness, the Basis for Faith

Speaking entirely from a natural perspective, if you were told by a well-known wealthy man that he was *able* to buy everyone who lives on your street a new automobile, there would very likely be no action on your part or on the part of any of your neighbors. Though you are certain that he had the ability to easily do so, you wouldn't go outside to see if he had put one in your driveway.

But if you were told that he not only could but that he also was *willing* to do so for anyone who sent him a letter and asked, it would be a different matter. Suddenly there is a basis for faith. You, along with the entire neighborhood, would be sending "letters of request," and the entire street would be checking their driveways for new cars.

For the child of God to merely say, "I know God can," does not display faith at all, or at least the full foundation or basis for faith. True faith is believing that God both can and that He is willing. Some will say, "Well, when it comes to healing, we should pray, 'If it be Your will.' After all, if that prayer was good enough for Jesus, it should be good enough for us."

Jesus certainly prayed such a prayer to the Father, but it was never in connection with healing a sick person. He healed all who came to Him. Jesus prayed, "Not as I will, but as You will," as He was agonizing in the Garden of Gethsemane. It was a prayer of dedication and consecration. He was dedicating and consecrating His life to follow through with the Father's plan of redemption, even if it meant going to the cross.

There are several types of prayer spoken of in the New Testament. Different prayers are to be used in different situations. There is the prayer of faith, the prayer of intercession, the prayer of agreement, and as we find Jesus praying in Gethsemane, the prayer of dedication and consecration (Matthew 26:39).

Are we ever instructed to pray such a prayer? Yes, it is found in James 4:13–15, which declares,

> [13]Come now, you who say, "Today or tomorrow we will go to such and such a city, spend a year there, buy and sell, and make a profit"; [14]whereas you do not know what will happen tomorrow. For what is your life? It is even a vapor that appears for a little time and then vanishes away. [15]Instead you ought to say, "If the Lord wills, we shall live and do this or that."

Like Jesus, we should submit the direction of our lives to the plans and purposes that the Father has ordained for us (Ephesians 2:10). However, Jesus never prayed such a prayer over a single sick person in all the days of His earthly ministry. What type of prayer then are we instructed to pray over the sick?

Again, we go to the book of James. Very clearly, we are instructed in 5:14–15,

> [14]Is anyone among you sick? Let him call for the elders of the church, and let them pray over him, anointing him with oil in the name of the Lord. [15]And the prayer of faith will save the sick, and the Lord will raise him up. And if he has committed sins, he will be forgiven.

We are to pray the prayer of faith for the sick, a prayer of confident expectation, which is based both on God's ability and His willingness.

Go Show Yourself to the Priest

> And He charged him to tell no one, "But go and show yourself to the priest, and make an offering for your cleansing, as a testimony to them, just as Moses commanded." (Luke 5:14)

When Jesus told the leper to go and show himself to the priest, He was telling him to let his healing be documented, even as it is stated in the law to do. Any healing that Jesus does today will stand up to medical scrutiny, and we shouldn't be afraid to get it verified.

Imagine when the priests inquired as to how he had been cured. He would have told them about Jesus. What a testimony to them! Jesus cures the man and is interested in fulfilling what the law requires in such cases, for He did not come to destroy the law, but to fulfill it.

Both Colossians 2:16–17 and Hebrews 10:1 teach us that the Old Testament truths and law were a shadow of things to come. They were, in many respects, types that pointed to the reality of Christ. The ceremony connected to the healing of a leper was one such shadow that pointed to "good things to come."

In Leviticus 14, where the law of the leper is recorded, we find that an atonement or sacrifice was made in connection with the cleansing of a leper. Two birds were to be brought, and one was to be killed. The blood was then to be sprinkled seven times on the healed man. The remaining live bird was to be dipped in the blood of the sacrificed bird and released.

What an example of Christ's sacrifice and God's provision! We are covered by the blood of the Son of God who died that we might go free! It represents His victory over both sin and sickness. As the instructions progress in Leviticus 14, we find that a lamb was to also be sacrificed.

This was all to be done because a man was healed. God wanted it forever ingrained in the hearts and minds of His people that healing was connected to the sacrifice of a lamb and to the shedding of its blood.

They were healed on the basis of Christ's coming sacrifice. This type and shadow pointed to the fact that Christ would pay a price for both our bodies and our spirits in His coming sacrifice (1 Corinthians 6:20). They were healed on the grounds of the atonement future while we are healed on the grounds of the atonement past (1 Peter 2:24).

Hear and Be Healed

Jesus charged the man who had been healed to tell no one, but rather go straight to the priest. Contrary to Jesus' strict warning, however, he went out and began to proclaim it freely and to spread the matter.

The result was that the crowds grew so large that Jesus could no longer openly enter the city (Mark 1:40–45). Luke 5:15 tells us about those crowds. It says,

> However, the report went around concerning Him all the more; and great multitudes came together to hear, and to be healed by Him of their infirmities.

It is noteworthy that the multitudes first came to **hear and then be healed**. We find a similar statement in Luke 6:17 where we are told that a great number of people came to Jesus "to hear and to be healed of their diseases." Wherever He went, Jesus' normal method of operation was to **teach**, **preach**, and then **heal** (Matthew 4:23; 9:35). The predominant reason for this is that "faith comes by hearing, and hearing by the word of God" (Romans 10:17).

In our fast-paced, frenetic society, many people do not have either the patience or the desire to hear. Even among those who name the name of Christ, the practice of unhurriedly listening to or meditating upon God's Word is becoming more and more rare. Many want to be prayed for, but they are not nearly as interested in hearing first. Even in churches that offer healing prayers for the sick, many times those prayers are prayed or hands are laid with little or no time spent in the Word first.

The Scriptures tell us that Paul saw that the cripple at Lystra "had faith to be healed" (and he was instantly healed). Where and how did he obtain that faith? It came from listening to Paul preach the good news about Jesus (Acts 14:7–10). He heard and was healed.

Crisis in the Back Country

Many years ago, I was on a backpacking trip with my dad and a couple of his friends. We had hiked to a very remote area in the High Sierras in California. We were so far back in the wilderness it would have taken two full days of hard hiking to get to the nearest ranger station.

Then it happened.

We had made camp and were heating some water over a fire when my dad pulled me aside. "We've got a serious problem. Jack* has a medical issue that needs attention now." It was then that I noticed Jack was not by the fire. I got up and found him sitting on a log, some distance from the camp.

I went and sat next to him, and his face was etched with fear and pain. He told me that he had an abdominal obstruction and that he had been hospitalized for the same thing recently. He said, "I'm in pain. I don't know what to do. I can't hike out, and if you did and they sent a helicopter in, I don't think I could last that long."

---

* Name changed for privacy.

I walked over to my pack, got out my pocket New Testament, and then went and sat beside Jack again.

"I want to share some Scriptures with you, and then I'm going to pray," I said. "Is that okay?" "Yes," he said, still in obvious pain.

I read him various passages and promises on the subject of healing and talked about the ministry of Jesus. I told him that Jesus was still the same compassionate Healer today that He was when He walked the shores of Galilee. I had him look in my New Testament and read several stories to me aloud about Jesus healing people.

When I sensed he was ready, I laid hands on his head and prayed. Within twenty minutes, he was back at the fire with the rest of us. He had been healed and experienced no further difficulties of that kind for the remainder of our week-long hike. I honestly don't believe he would have experienced healing if he first hadn't been willing to hear.

The Word Doing Its Work

A group of students from the Bible college at our church traveled down to Mexico to participate in a gospel crusade being held by a Mexican evangelist we often worked with and supported. When those students returned, they were thrilled. They had been kept busy praying for people and helping with different aspects of the nightly meetings. They witnessed scores come to faith in Christ and saw a number of miraculous healings take place before their eyes. One story of healing that they shared really stood out to me.

They said that on the first night of the crusade a father brought his young adult son to be prayed for. The young man had some crippling disease and required constant assistance. To the father's dismay, instead of praying for the young man, the evangelist told him to bring his boy back every night to hear the preaching. The father was angry. Why not pray for him now? It will be hard to bring him every night. With all of the assistance he requires, it won't be easy to get him here. But the evangelist refused to pray and flatly told the father, "Just bring him."

Reluctantly, the father complied, helping his son into the service each night to hear the preaching. On the third night something miraculous happened. At the end of the preaching, before prayer for the sick was offered, that young man suddenly stood up on his own, completely unassisted, and began shouting and praising God. He was healed, and his physical transformation had been dramatic. The father was beside himself with joy, and the entire gathering, upon realizing what had happened, broke out into spontaneous praise and shouting themselves.

Observing that young man's healing deeply affected our Bible school students. They had a firsthand experience of the power of God's Word. The evangelist had told them that the reason he didn't pray for the young man on the first night was because he inwardly sensed that he wasn't ready. He needed to hear the Word so that his faith could come alive.

Well, it had come alive. That young man listened to the gospel and, like the man at Lystra, had faith to be healed. Without anyone praying for him, he believed and embraced the message. He experienced a demonstration of Psalm 107:20, which says, "**He sent His word and healed them.**"

Take the Time to Hear

Dear reader, if you are in need of healing, take the time to hear. Prayerfully and unhurriedly read through the Gospel of Luke (or any of the Gospels). Let the seed of God's Word find a home and take root in your heart. It would be unrealistic to expect a harvest where no seed has been planted. The time you take listening to and meditating on God's promises is never wasted time. The time you take to closely watch and listen to Jesus as He deals with the sick during His earthly ministry will build a robust faith in your heart.

Also, as we take the time to hear and wait upon God, He often deals with wrong thinking and wrong attitudes that are hindering us from receiving all that He has for us. If you were scheduled to have a major surgery, you wouldn't show up to the hospital ten minutes beforehand, expecting them to wheel you into the operating room right then and there. It wouldn't matter if you had a busy schedule or not.

More than likely, you would have to eat a special diet for a few days prior to the scheduled surgery. They likely would require you to check in to the hospital the day before, and on the day of surgery they would make sure you were bathed and clean and that the area where the surgery was to take place was completely sterilized.

How is it that we acquiesce to the wisdom of such natural practices and yet cannot take the time to prepare ourselves for the Great Physician? Dare we come to Him saying, "I'm in a hurry. I have things to do. I don't have time to listen to Your Word or the desire to let it wash me clean. Just do Your work so I can be on my way" (John 17:17; Ephesians 5:26)?

Like one old preacher said, "It takes longer to lay down the track than it does for the train to roll through." Taking the time to hear is equivalent to laying the track. The train of healing can roll through suddenly, but it is not likely where no track has been laid.

Postscript

Jesus has been teaching, preaching, and healing. He has been giving out to the multitudes who are now seeking Him. He is the Son of God, but as we talked about in the first chapter, He now, by His own choice, has the limitations of living in a human body. The demand upon Him spiritually, emotionally, and physically was great. What did He do to replenish Himself? He withdrew often into the wilderness and prayed (Luke 5:16). If Jesus needed to often withdraw in order to spend undistracted time with His Father, do we not need to do the same?

CHAPTER

3

The Power of the Lord Was Present

[17]Now it happened on a certain day, as He was teaching, that there were Pharisees and teachers of the law sitting by, who had come out of every town of Galilee, Judea, and Jerusalem. And the power of the Lord was present to heal them. [18]Then behold, men brought on a bed a man who was paralyzed, whom they sought to bring in and lay before Him. [19]And when they could not find how they might bring him in, because of the crowd, they went up on the housetop and let him down with his bed through the tiling into the midst before Jesus.

[20]When He saw their faith, He said to him, "Man, your sins are forgiven you."

[21]And the scribes and the Pharisees began to reason, saying, "Who is this who speaks blasphemies? Who can forgive sins but God alone?"

²²But when Jesus perceived their thoughts, He answered and said to them, "Why are you reasoning in your hearts? ²³Which is easier, to say, 'Your sins are forgiven you,' or to say, 'Rise up and walk'? ²⁴But that you may know that the Son of Man has power on earth to forgive sins"—He said to the man who was paralyzed, "I say to you, arise, take up your bed, and go to your house."

²⁵Immediately he rose up before them, took up what he had been lying on, and departed to his own house, glorifying God. ²⁶And they were all amazed, and they glorified God and were filled with fear, saying, "We have seen strange things today!" (Luke 5:17–26)

This is an amazing story that is filled with relevant truth for those who are seeking healing today. I would like to point out seven things from this story that I believe are worthy of our deepest consideration.

1. We can bring others to Jesus for healing.

We wouldn't have this remarkable story if not for the men who brought the paralyzed man on a bed. He could not have come on his own. It was only through their assistance that he was able to reach Jesus.

First and foremost, we can bring others to Christ in prayer. Only eternity will tell the effect that our prayers have had in this world. James 5:16 says, "pray for one another, that you may be healed." In a physical, practical sense, we can bring our friends and acquaintances to church or to a meeting where prayer for the sick is being offered.

Back in the early days of our church, when we were still meeting in a small, rented building, two women brought a friend of theirs for prayer. Back then, every Sunday night we taught on healing and prayed for the sick. Their friend had suffered from terrible, debilitating migraine headaches every day.

The evening they brought her she had a severe one. After listening to the preaching, her friends brought her forward for prayer. She was instantly healed when hands were laid on her. She began to sob the moment the pain left her head. When she stopped crying I asked her if she wanted to ask Christ into her heart (she was not a Christian).

Without hesitation she said, "Yes!" I led her in a sinner's prayer and then explained that Jesus also wanted to baptize her in the Holy Spirit. "I want it all!" she said. In five minutes she was standing there, pain free, arms raised, tears streaming down her cheeks, and speaking in other tongues.

She became a devoted member of the church and was never visited by those migraine headaches again. It was an amazing story of God's grace, but none of it would have happened if her friends had not brought her.

2. They didn't quit when they ran into obstacles.

Think of the trial these guys had in getting their friend to Jesus. Some would have said, "If it's the Lord's will for him to be healed, there will be an open door. We'll get a seat up front." No, they got there and couldn't even get in the house because of the crowd. It says "they could not find how they might bring him in" (v. 19), meaning they tried. Front door . . . no luck, too crowded. Back door . . . same thing. Asking people to move out of the way and let them pass by so they could get to Jesus . . . "No way!" responded the crowd. "You should have gotten here earlier!"

Many people would have turned around and gone home, but they were determined. ***Real faith is tenacious***. They actually climbed up on the roof looking for a way in and they hauled their paralyzed friend up there as well. Finally, they tore the tiles off of the roof! Imagine the scene inside! Jesus is teaching when suddenly He is interrupted by loud banging and debris and dust falling on everyone's head. The hole above them keeps getting bigger and bigger until finally, a man on a bed is lowered down before Jesus.

People had to move out of the way to give room to the man and his bed. Jesus was not angry (though maybe the owner of the house was). A dust-covered Jesus looked at the man on the bed and at his friends peering down through the roof they had just ruined, and the Scripture says, "He saw their faith" (v. 20)! Faith is an act. Faith without actions is dead (James 2:20, 26). They acted and they refused to quit because they believed!

Dear friend, the fact that they faced obstacles was no indication that it was not the Lord's will for the paralyzed man to be healed. These men did not take the barriers they faced as some sign that God was not in what they were doing. Jesus proved it was the Father's will for the man to be healed because He healed him! Yet, if not for the tenacious faith of these men, this story would not be in the Bible.

3. Jesus forgave his sins.

They came seeking healing, but the first thing Jesus did was to declare that the paralyzed man's sins were forgiven. Apparently it was important for this man to know that before he could be healed. First John 3:21 declares, "If our heart does not condemn us, we have confidence toward God." There is no doubt that a guilty conscience has robbed many of their confidence in prayer or in seeking God for some promised benefit.

How good it is to know that the blood of Jesus can even cleanse a guilty conscience, and that "if we confess our sins He is faithful and just to forgive our sins and to cleanse us from all unrighteousness" (Hebrews 9:14; 1 John 1:9).

God Must Hate Me

When I was a new believer, I spent an afternoon with a friend in a local park. As I told her about what Jesus had done for me, she suddenly began to cry. "What's wrong?" I asked her. "Bayless, I've never told you this, but before I met you, I had two abortions. I killed two of my unborn children. God must hate me!"

I was stunned. I didn't know what to tell her. I do believe that abortion is murder, but I was also certain that God didn't hate her. "I don't think God hates you. He loves you," I told her. "No, He must hate me for what I did," she said through her tears.

As I said, I was a new believer. Back then I didn't know that God had said, "As far as the east is from the west, so far has He removed our transgressions from us" (Psalm 103:12), or that *He would forgive our iniquity and remember our sin no more* (Jeremiah 31:34). To my friend, her sin and the resulting guilty conscience she had because of it stood as an impenetrable barrier between her and the goodness of God.

You might be thinking, *Okay pastor, I can understand that, but this guy in the story was a paralytic! How much sin can someone who is paralyzed commit? It's not likely that they could commit murder or adultery or even theft. So what's the deal?*

Why did he need to hear Jesus say, "*Your sins are forgiven you*" (v. 20)? Because all sins are not outward. There are inward sins as well, and they can be just as damaging to our conscience and can hinder our confidence in God just as surely as outward transgressions. Anger, bitterness, and lust are a few examples.

The good news is that our God is rich in mercy to all who call upon Him, and if you think about it, only the guilty need mercy! Psalm 130:3–4 says, "If You, Lord, should mark iniquities, O Lord, who could stand? But there is forgiveness with You, that You may be feared."

Dear friend, if your conscience is heavy, laden with guilt, take your burden to the One who can set you free. Confess your sin to God and trust in the cleansing power of Christ's precious blood. Then listen to the Spirit whisper to your heart, *"Your sins are forgiven you."*

4. The ones whom the power of the Lord was present to heal did not get healed.

It was the will of the Lord to heal the Pharisees and teachers of the law who were sitting by (and had come out of every town of Galilee, Judea, and Jerusalem), and it was obvious that some of them were sick. The power of God was present to heal (v. 17). Yet none of them were healed.

By contrast, the paralytic, who was not among those whom the power of the Lord was present to heal (he came on the scene later), was healed. He was healed, and those whom the power of the Lord was present to heal received nothing. Why? The short answer is because they *reasoned* and he had *faith* (vv. 20–22).

They were *sitting by*, not sitting at His feet to be taught. They said preach *before us* but not *to us*. They were not there to receive but to scrutinize and to try and catch Him in His words. It was much like the people in Jeremiah's day who said,

> Come, let us devise plans against Jeremiah. . . . Come and let us attack him with the tongue, and let us not give heed to any of his words. (Jeremiah 18:18)

They sat and questioned while the paralytic and his friends acted.

That same poisonous attitude of heart is still around today. On a number of occasions throughout the years, I have attended meetings where divine healing was being taught and where the sick were being prayed for (in some of them I was the one doing the preaching). And there have been both those with legitimate needs and hungry hearts as well as the *scrutinizers* in attendance.

Those who came to scrutinize generally had already made up their minds on the subject and were not open to any teaching that contradicted their beliefs, no matter how scripturally sound that teaching was.

Their hearts were closed and their only reason for attending was to take some snippet of the sermon or some lone statement to use as *proof* that the minister was teaching error and should be avoided. On rare occasions they had come with the sole purpose of disrupting the meetings.

And just like with those Pharisees and teachers of the law in the house with Jesus, even though because of God's great mercy His power was present to heal them, they received nothing at all.

5. The same power that forgives sins heals disease.

> 23"Which is easier, to say, 'Your sins are forgiven you,' or to say, 'Rise up and walk'? 24But that you may know that the Son of Man has power on earth to forgive sins"—He said to the man who was paralyzed, "I say to you, arise, take up your bed, and go to your house."
>
> 25Immediately he rose up before them, took up what he had been lying on, and departed to his own house, glorifying God. (Luke 5:23–25)

What an amazing lesson! The religious leaders rightly believed that sin and sickness were connected. Before sin entered the world there was no sickness, and when the devil and sin are removed from the scene, sickness, pain, and suffering will be eliminated as well (Revelation 21:4).

They knew, though they likely would not admit it, that if Jesus could heal disease He could also forgive sin because they both have the same origin.

Something Unusual Happened

I listened to an old preacher tell an illuminating story about one of his contemporaries. It seems that the man he was speaking about was a great evangelist. He had won thousands to Christ around the world. He preached a straightforward salvation message and saw amazing results. After all, faith comes by hearing, and if we talk about Jesus as the Savior from sin, it will produce faith in the hearts of the hearers.

This evangelist was brilliant at preaching forgiveness, but he never preached on healing. He wasn't against it, it was just that he preached what he knew and stayed with the message that he felt God had called him to preach.

In one meeting, he chose Isaiah 53 as his text. In the course of preaching his salvation message, he brought out the literal Hebrew definitions in verse 4 where it says *surely He (Jesus) has borne our sicknesses and carried our pains*. Hundreds came to faith in Christ that night. It was a great success.

But something unusual happened. Reports began to come in that a number of people were physically healed when they put their trust in Christ. The evangelist's response was to say, "*I think there is a lot more to Isaiah 53 than we previously thought!*" I am persuaded that he was correct in making that statement. And the more we preach about Jesus being the Healer as well as the Savior from sin, the more we will hear about healings taking place. Faith for healing and faith for forgiveness both come by hearing.

Sozo

Luke 7:48–50 tells us about a sinner whom Jesus forgave. It says,

> ⁴⁸Then He said to her, "Your sins are forgiven." ⁴⁹And those who sat at the table with Him began to say to themselves, "Who is this who even forgives sins?" ⁵⁰Then He said to the woman, "Your faith has saved you. Go in peace."

When Jesus said your faith has saved you, the Greek word translated "saved" is *sozo*, and it is obviously talking about the forgiveness of sins. It is the most common word for salvation in the New Testament.

We find that same word used in the next chapter as well, and as we consider it, it becomes clear that God's idea of salvation extends beyond the forgiveness of sins. In telling the story of a demon-possessed man that Jesus delivered and restored to being in his right mind we read,

> ³⁵Then they went out to see what had happened, and came to Jesus, and found the man from whom the demons had departed, sitting at the feet of Jesus, clothed and in his right mind. And they were afraid. ³⁶They also who had seen it told them by what means he who had been demon-possessed was healed. (Luke 8:35–36)

The Greek word translated "healed" in verse 36 is *sozo*. So God's idea of salvation also encompasses freedom from demon powers. He has made provision for our minds as well as our bodies.

A few verses later in Luke 8, we find the story of a woman who had a flow of blood for twelve years. She had been impoverished by spending all she had on doctors, but none could help her. Having heard about Jesus, she made her way through a large crowd and grabbed the hem of His garment. When she did, she was instantly healed.

As Dr. Luke relates the story of her healing, he very carefully chooses a precise word to describe what happened to her. Jesus said to the woman, "Daughter, be of good cheer; your faith has made you well" (Luke 8:48).

The Greek word translated "made you well," which is distinctly speaking of physical healing in this case, is again *sozo*. So we see that God's idea of salvation extends yet further to include physical healing. Freedom from sin for the spirit of man, peace for the mind of man, and healing for the body of man. He is the complete Savior for all three realms of human existence.

Jesus proved that He had the power to forgive sins (which in the heart of man are unseen) by healing a sick man's body (which could be seen). All sickness is the indirect result of man's sin in the garden, and sometimes it is the direct result of personal sin (John 5:14). But Jesus is the master of both sin and sickness. He is our Forgiver and our Healer.

6. You have a right to go directly to Jesus.

In our story from Luke 5:17–25, we find that in the house where Jesus was there was such a crowd that no one else could fit inside. It seems that the majority of that crowd consisted of the religious elite. Pharisees and teachers of the law from far and wide had come and crowded into that house. There was a donkey taking up every parking space outside and wall to wall people inside. It was so full that no real seekers could get inside to have an encounter with Jesus.

There they sat. Minds already made up about Him. Hearts closed. Along come the men carrying the paralytic on his bed and they can't get in. The religious scholars are literally barring his way. So what do they do? The same thing you have a right to do with anyone who is barring your way from reaching the Savior and Healer. *They went over their heads!*

There is one mediator between God and men, the man Christ Jesus. We don't need to go through a priest or any other person (regardless of their title) to get access to the Lord. Every person can go directly to Him themselves! If any man or religious system is trying to prevent you from getting directly to Jesus, you can *go over their heads* to a higher authority. Come directly to the throne of grace to obtain mercy in your time of need (1 Timothy 2:5; Hebrews 4:16; John 6:37).

7. Healing glorifies God.

After he was healed, the previously paralyzed man departed to his own house *glorifying God*. When the crowd saw the healing miracle take place, they *glorified God* (vv. 25–26).

It was healing and not sickness that glorified God. We certainly understand that a person's attitude when suffering with a physical malady can glorify God, but to say that the sickness is what glorifies God is not what we find in the ministry of Jesus or in the Scriptures.

Consider these passages:

- [30]"Then great multitudes came to Him, having with them the lame, blind, mute, maimed, and many others; and they laid them down at Jesus' feet, and He healed them. [31]So the multitude marveled when they saw the mute speaking, the maimed made whole, the lame walking, and the blind seeing; **and they glorified the God of Israel**" (Matthew 15:30–31, emphasis mine).

- [10]"Now He was teaching in one of the synagogues on the Sabbath. [11]And behold, there was a woman who had a spirit of infirmity eighteen years, and was bent over and could in no way raise herself up. [12]But when Jesus saw her, He called her to Him and said to her, 'Woman, you are loosed from your infirmity.' [13]And He laid His hands on her, and immediately she was made straight, ***and glorified God*** (Luke 13:10–13, emphasis mine).

- ³⁵"Then it happened, as He was coming near Jericho, that a certain blind man sat by the road begging. ³⁶And hearing a multitude passing by, he asked what it meant. ³⁷So they told him that Jesus of Nazareth was passing by. ³⁸And he cried out, saying, 'Jesus, Son of David, have mercy on me!' ³⁹Then those who went before warned him that he should be quiet; but he cried out all the more, 'Son of David, have mercy on me!' ⁴⁰So Jesus stood still and commanded him to be brought to Him. And when he had come near, He asked him, ⁴¹saying, 'What do you want Me to do for you?' He said, 'Lord, that I may receive my sight.' ⁴²Then Jesus said to him, 'Receive your sight; your faith has made you well.' ⁴³And immediately he received his sight, and followed Him, ***glorifying God. And all the people, when they saw it, gave praise to God***" (Luke 18:35–43, emphasis mine).

- ²¹"So when they had further threatened them, they let them go, finding no way of punishing them, because of the people, since ***they all glorified God for what had been done***. ²²For the man was over forty years old on whom this miracle of healing had been performed" (Acts 4:21–22, emphasis mine).

Even with the death of Lazarus recorded in John 11, Jesus was not glorified when Lazarus was sick or when he died, but only when he was raised. In all of the other Scriptures we listed it is the same. Jesus is glorified through healing and when His power is displayed. Let us endeavor to maintain sweet demeanors and clean hearts if we are suffering physically, but let us also fill our hearts with the promises, putting our trust in the One who can raise us up.

CHAPTER

4

A Miracle in the Synagogue

No Excuses for Not Attending Church

Jesus had recently had a run-in with some of the Pharisees regarding the Sabbath (Luke 6:1–5). Their harsh and legalistic interpretation of the Sabbath was not even close to what God had originally intended.

Now, we find Jesus going into their synagogue on another Sabbath (Matthew 12:9). These are the same guys who had just picked a fight with Him! By going into their house of worship right after they had been so unkind to Him teaches us the importance of church attendance. I have known several people through the years who blame their lack of church attendance on the fact that there are hypocrites in God's house or because someone had treated them unfairly or unkindly.

Let us follow the example of Jesus and faithfully turn out for worship and instruction in the Word, regardless of how we have been treated by church leaders or other members of the congregation.

First Line of Defense or Last-Ditch Effort?

> ⁶Now it happened on another Sabbath, also, that He entered the synagogue and taught. And a man was there whose right hand was withered. ⁷So the scribes and Pharisees watched Him closely, whether He would heal on the Sabbath, that they might find an accusation against Him. ⁸But He knew their thoughts, and said to the man who had the withered hand, "Arise and stand here." And he arose and stood. ⁹Then Jesus said to them, "I will ask you one thing: Is it lawful on the Sabbath to do good or to do evil, to save life or to destroy?" ¹⁰And when He had looked around at them all, He said to the man, "Stretch out your hand." And he did so, and his hand was restored as whole as the other. ¹¹But they were filled with rage, and discussed with one another what they might do to Jesus. (Luke 6:6–11)

The first thing that Jesus did upon entering the synagogue was not to heal—it was to teach. For those who are seeking healing from the Lord, this is an important point to consider. We should be hungry for knowledge and seek to be taught before we seek to be healed. Faith comes by hearing and hearing by the Word of God (Romans 10:17).

In much of the world where medical care is available, most people will devote a large amount of time and resources to their physical health. For example, a person who becomes ill will take time off from work to go and see a doctor. They will either drive or find transportation to the doctor's office. When they arrive, they will sit in a waiting room for approximately a half hour or more until their name is called. Then they are escorted to a private room where they will wait for maybe another ten or fifteen minutes until the doctor comes in to see them.

After being examined and perhaps having several tests run, they will listen carefully to the doctor's diagnosis after which he or she will generally write them a prescription for a particular medication. The doctor may ask them to make another appointment in a week to come back and see him or her, which they gladly do. They take the time to go to a pharmacy to get their prescription filled and then diligently take the medication according to the directions.

This is all pretty standard, at least for many living in the United States or other developed countries. Much time and perhaps money is spent on the prospect of getting well, and people usually hang on every word their doctor says when it comes to their recovery.

How is it then that when a person is willing to devote so much time, money, and attention to a natural physician and to natural means of recovery that they cannot seem to find the time or attention to give to the Great Physician? If we would devote the same amount of time, attention, and resources to listening to the words of the Great Physician as we do to natural doctors and medical professionals, we would see and experience far greater results than we ever have before when it comes to divine healing.

For many, going to the Lord for healing is not their *first line of defense* when attacked with sickness. It is usually their *last-ditch effort* after every human and natural avenue of recovery has failed them. Certainly our God is merciful in such cases, but He is not honored when we come to Him last.

Dear friend, take the time to hear His Word on the subject of healing. Search the Scriptures and unhurriedly meditate upon the promises that speak of physical healing. It will not be a wasted investment of your time, attention, or resources.

They Watched Him Closely

The scribes and Pharisees watched Jesus closely, not to see if He could help a poor member of their congregation who had been severely handicapped, but to try and find a reason to accuse Him. They were about to get a lesson on the Sabbath that they would never forget.

If He healed the man with the withered hand, the scribes and Pharisees were going to accuse Jesus of violating one of the Ten Commandments by working on the Sabbath. Their interpretation of God's command to rest was twisted and harsh because their own hearts were twisted and harsh. As well as having compassion for the poor man by healing him, Jesus used him as an object lesson to reveal the true spirit of the Sabbath.

Jesus asked them whether it was lawful to do good or evil, to save life or to destroy it on the Sabbath. In so doing, Jesus is telling us that healing and the restoration of life are good, not evil. Numerous times in Scripture, disease and sickness are referred to as being evil. Sickness destroys life. Jesus clearly stated elsewhere that it is the enemy's work to kill, steal, and destroy, while He came to bring us abundant life (John 10:10).

Acts 10:38 declares, "God anointed Jesus of Nazareth with the Holy Spirit and with power, who went about doing good and healing all who were oppressed by the devil, for God was with Him."

According to this verse, healing is good and sickness is a form of satanic oppression. We know that there was no sickness in the world until the devil showed up, just like there was no sin. The twin evils of sin and sickness can both be attributed (either directly or indirectly) to the intrusion of Satan into God's creation. It was both lawful and right to undo the enemy's work on the Sabbath by healing the man's withered hand.

Stretch Out Your Hand

Jesus told the man to stretch out his withered hand, and when he did it was completely restored. Many times Jesus told the sick to perform some act in connection with their healing. Whether it was, "Take up your bed," or "Stretch out your hand," or "Go to the pool and wash," it was significant. Faith must be accompanied by *corresponding actions* (James 2:18 WNT).

In Hebrews 11, we are given a long list of people that did exploits and received miracles by faith. As we read through that archive, one thing is very clear: their faith was expressed through action. To mention a few: by faith Abel *offered his first and his best*, Noah *prepared*, Abraham *obeyed and went out*, Sarah *received*, and Moses *refused, chose, and forsook*. Their faith was expressed, or we could say *it was released* through their actions.

An Octopus on My Back

Years ago I went on a spearfishing trip with some friends to the Sea of Cortez in Mexico. We were free diving and having great success in spearing our two main target fish: yellowtail and cabrilla. One afternoon as I was diving along some rock structure at a depth of about fifteen feet, I saw a very large octopus. I grabbed it and swam for the surface.

By the time my head popped out of the water and I had the chance to gulp down a lungful of air, things had changed dramatically. I no longer had the octopus. He had me.

It's hard to describe the strength of a large octopus if you have not experienced it. I still had a grip on it, but it had somehow shifted most of its body around to my back. Try as I might, I could not dislodge it. As I was treading water with this creature clinging solidly to my body, I called out to one of my friends who was diving nearby for some help. It was only by both of us working together and using all of our strength that we finally peeled the octopus off of my back.

If someone had witnessed the wrestling match between me and my eight-armed nemesis, they might have called out, "Hang on to him, Bayless!" The truth was that I was not trying to hang on to him. I was trying to turn him loose! That's what we need to do with our faith—turn it loose! Let it go to God. And the way we do that is through action.

Filled with Rage

It is amazing to think that the scribes and Pharisees were not filled with joy over the miracle that had occurred. A member of their own flock was healed. They would have known him and his family. They knew that his options in life had been severely limited due to his unfortunate physical condition. They knew that he would have had to endure the whispers that God must have punished him for some sin that he or his parents had committed, a common belief of the time.

Now, right before their eyes, he is made whole! Are they happy? No, they are filled with rage! They had no compassion for the man. They didn't care that he had been healed. They didn't care about his family and how this blessing would translate into good things for them as he would now be able to do work that he previously could not have done. They didn't gather to discuss the amazing display of mercy and power they had just seen. Instead, they immediately began to plan how they might harm Jesus.

There are religious people today whose minds work the same way. Their thoughts are set on criticizing those who are active in the healing ministry, and if they hear of (or see) someone receive the benefit of healing, they do not rejoice. They look for reasons to bring accusation. In Mark's account of this story, it says that Jesus "*looked around at them with anger, being grieved by the hardness of their hearts*"

(Mark 3:5). That kind of attitude angered and grieved Jesus then and it still does today.

Jesus, though saddened and angered by the words and actions of these heartless critics, carried on with His mission of teaching and healing. After choosing twelve men from His disciples and calling them apostles, we read,

> [17]He came down with them and stood on a level place with a crowd of His disciples and a great multitude of people from all Judea and Jerusalem, and from the seacoast of Tyre and Sidon, who came to hear Him and be healed of their diseases, [18]as well as those who were tormented with unclean spirits. And they were healed. [19]And the whole multitude sought to touch Him, for power went out from Him and healed them all. (Luke 6:17–19)

Again, we see that the people came to *hear and be healed*. Jesus taught them and they listened. Healing power went out from Him and healed them all.

The Healer Came Down

Verse 17 states, *"He came down."* From reading the previous verses, we see that it was from the mountain where He had been praying and where He had chosen the Twelve, but the language makes one think on a grander scale. He came down, not just from the mountain, but from heaven!

He didn't have to, but He did. He left the glories of heaven and came to this sin-sick world to rescue us. When I couldn't reach Him, He reached me. When I was in need, lost, confused, sick, oppressed, and crushed under the enemy's heel, the Lord was in heaven, above it all, but He was touched with the feelings of my infirmity *and He came down*! In all of my affliction, He was afflicted and He came down!

The story is told that General George Washington was riding down a road with one of his officers one snowy day. They came upon a wagon that had lost its load of wood. Several privates struggled to lift a large log back on the bed of the wagon as their superior officer yelled at them to get their backs into their work. Because of the heavy overcoat covering his uniform, General Washington was not recognized by the man yelling at his subordinates.

Washington immediately stepped down from his horse and put his shoulder into the load, helping the men to lift the log. "And who are you, sir?!" demanded the one who had yelled and not helped. "I am General Washington, the commander of this army," came the reply.

Our God has done the same. He stepped down from His lofty place of habitation to lift our burden! The commander of the armies of heaven condescended to our low estate and rescued us. He humbled Himself, accepting the role of a servant and taking on human form. The Word became flesh and dwelt among us.

When praying, don't talk and act as if God is beyond the farthest reaches of space. He has come down! Romans 10:6 says, "But the righteousness of faith speaks in this way, 'Do not say in your heart, "Who will ascend into heaven?"' (that is, to bring Christ down from above)."

Why? Because He has already come down! And now the Word is near us, even in our mouth and in our heart (Romans 10:8).

I had a friend living on the other side of the US who was in trouble. I got on a plane and flew two thousand miles to help him. But Jesus came all the way from heaven to help us! Dear friend, don't ever think that God is not moved by your suffering. Don't even entertain the idea that He might not care. He was so moved that He took upon Himself human flesh to reach you and help you.

He Stood on a Level Place

Verse 17 also tells us that "He stood on a level place" where everyone had equal access. Again, the language takes one's thoughts beyond the marvels that were taking place that day to an even larger truth. He still stands on a level place. It is a level playing field, so to speak. There is no advantage to being rich or poor, Caucasian, Black, Hispanic, Asian, or Pacific Islander. The field is level. God plays no favorites. He is no respecter of persons.

Romans 10:10–13 tells us,

> [10]For with the heart one believes unto righteousness, and with the mouth confession is made unto salvation. [11]For the Scripture says, "Whoever believes on Him will not be put to shame." [12]For there is no distinction between Jew and Greek, for the same Lord over all is rich to all who call upon Him. [13]For "whoever calls on the name of the Lord shall be saved."

Romans 4:16 and 5:1–2 tell us plainly that faith gives us access into His grace, not our looks, education, upbringing, natural ability, or ethnic background!

He came and stood on a level place where anyone who seeks Him can reach Him. It makes no difference if you are a businessman in Los Angeles or a village woman in Ethiopia. Jesus, the Healer, is accessible by all!

CHAPTER

5

Great Faith

There are only two occasions in Scripture where Jesus marveled: one was at someone's faith and the other was at a group of people's unbelief (Luke 7:9; Mark 6:6).

We are now going to take a look at a most illuminating story. A servant will be healed, genuine humility and faith are found working in tandem, and Jesus is going to marvel at and admire the faith of an outsider.

> ¹Now when He concluded all His sayings in the hearing of the people, He entered Capernaum. ²And a certain centurion's servant, who was dear to him, was sick and ready to die. ³So when he heard about Jesus, he sent elders of the Jews to Him, pleading with Him to come and heal his servant. ⁴And when they came to Jesus, they begged Him earnestly, saying that the one for whom He should do this was deserving, ⁵"for he loves our nation, and has built us a synagogue."

⁶Then Jesus went with them. And when He was already not far from the house, the centurion sent friends to Him, saying to Him, "Lord, do not trouble Yourself, for I am not worthy that You should enter under my roof. ⁷Therefore I did not even think myself worthy to come to You. But say the word, and my servant will be healed. ⁸For I also am a man placed under authority, having soldiers under me. And I say to one, 'Go,' and he goes; and to another, 'Come,' and he comes; and to my servant, 'Do this,' and he does it."

⁹When Jesus heard these things, He marveled at him, and turned around and said to the crowd that followed Him, "I say to you, I have not found such great faith, not even in Israel!" ¹⁰And those who were sent, returning to the house, found the servant well who had been sick. (Luke 7:1–10)

Six Things to Consider

This story is absolutely full of important lessons when it comes to faith and healing, and although there are certainly more lessons that can be drawn from this account, I will limit my musings to six.

1. Someone was a faithful ambassador.

This whole story would be absent from the Holy Writ if some unknown, unnamed person had not shared what they knew or had heard about Jesus. Verse 3 says that when the centurion *"heard about Jesus, he sent elders of the Jews to Him."* Did he hear about Jesus from a friend or family member? Was it from one of his servants or from a fellow soldier? We are not told, but someone, by telling him about Jesus, opened the door for this great healing miracle to take place.

It was the same with the woman who was healed of the flow of blood and with the healing of Naaman the Syrian. Someone spoke up and it gave birth to faith in the heart (Mark 5:25–29; 2 Kings 5:2–4). Proverbs 13:17 declares, "***A faithful ambassador brings health***." Second Corinthians 5:20 tells us that as believers, "we are ambassadors for Christ." It is important as His representatives that we herald both His willingness and His ability to forgive and to heal (Psalm 103:1–3).

A Wretched Life Turned Beautiful

As a young Christian, I spent some time helping with a large evangelistic campaign in Mexico. Nightly, the evangelist leading the campaign preached the gospel and prayed for the sick. Scores were healed and huge crowds embraced Christ as their Savior.

The meetings, which were being held in an outdoor area, were growing and gaining momentum as word joyfully spread of all that God was doing. Things, however, came to a grinding halt one day when the local police came and shut the meetings down. The reason for the forced closure was that the evangelist was *practicing medicine without a license*. At least that was the reason they gave.

The meeting that night was moved to a town about twenty miles south and was held in a small church. Somehow the crowds heard about the move and they showed up. The little church building was filled to overflowing and people were standing several deep outside as they listened at the windows. Many put their faith in Jesus and many were healed, but something occurred that first night at the new location that I shall never forget.

Several people brought a woman who looked like a living skeleton. Her face was etched with pain and she was so weak she could barely walk. Later we found out that she had been in that condition for a long time and had been in constant, almost unbearable pain. At the conclusion of the message, she was brought forward to be prayed for. The moment the evangelist laid his hand on her head a look of shock and joy erupted on her face. She cried and she laughed as she testified that all of the pain had suddenly left and she knew that Jesus had healed her.

She came back every night to the meetings, which lasted another four days, and testified about her healing. She no longer needed assistance, her countenance changed dramatically, she was pain-free, and she put on weight every day because for the first time in months she could eat and keep her food down.

It was amazing to see and hear firsthand, and to this day I am grateful for the mercies that God bestowed upon her. But there is something I also keep in mind every time I think of what God did for her that night . . . someone had to have told her about the meetings and what God was doing. A wretched, bitter, pain-wracked life was turned beautiful and sweet because someone had acted as a faithful ambassador for Christ.

2. The motive for the request

The centurion did not request healing for his servant because he had invested a lot of time and resources into his training and it would be hard to replace him. He did not request healing so he would look good, find favor, or appear to be compassionate to anyone. The reason he sought out Jesus to heal his servant was because the man "was dear to him" (v. 2). It could be translated that the servant was *precious* to him.

It is important that we see people as valuable and precious. God thought that we were so valuable and precious that He sent His Son to die for us. He had nothing to gain personally from our redemption. He could always raise up new sons and daughters from the stones if He wanted to.

The simple truth is that God loves us and He has our welfare at heart. In Matthew's account, the centurion relayed to Jesus that his servant was *dreadfully tormented*. He had compassion, and as uncommon as it might have been in that culture, circumstance, and time, he loved and genuinely cared for his servant. His desire to see him healed had nothing to do with personal gain, comfort, or reputation. His motive for asking was totally unselfish.

The Scripture teaches us, "And even when you ask, you don't get it because your motives are all wrong—you want only what will give you pleasure" (James 4:3 NLT). Not as a matter of overanalyzing our motives when we pray, but as a common-sense practice, we should, from time to time, honestly ask ourselves, "Why am I praying for the things I have brought before God?" If God reveals an impure motive, repent and correct it. If nothing is amiss, carry on with confidence.

3. The clarity of the request

There was nothing vague about the centurion's request. It was very specific and to the point. He wanted Jesus to "come and heal his servant" (v. 3). He didn't send the elders of the Jews with an unspoken request (something that you don't find anywhere in Scripture), and he didn't ask for some unspecified blessing. Yet, many times you find believers doing just that. Unspoken requests are prayed over regularly in some church services and vague, unspecified blessings are often asked for. Try that the next time you go to your local bank. After entering the bank, go up to a teller and tell them that you have an unspoken request. See how far you get!

He Knows Before I Ask Him

After I had been saved a few weeks, I ran into an old friend. After talking for a few minutes, I was delighted to find out that he had also come to faith in Christ. In fact, he had been saved for a whole year! As a brand-new believer, to me, that seemed like a very long time. I couldn't even imagine what it would be like to walk with God and study His Word for a whole year. I was impressed!

As we walked and talked that evening, he said to me, "You know, Bayless, I never ask God for anything."

"Really?" I responded with genuine amazement. "Why?"

"Because Jesus said that the Father already knows what I need before I ask Him. So because He already knows, there is no reason for me to ask." Again, I was impressed.

I thought a lot about what he said, and the more I thought about it the more it bothered me inside. Something didn't feel right about it, so I began to search the Scriptures to see just exactly what he had founded his conclusion upon. It didn't take me long to find it. In Matthew 6:8 Jesus said, "For your Father knows the things you have need of before you ask Him." But the very next thing that Jesus said in verse 9 is, "In this manner therefore pray," meaning that even though God knows our needs we still need to ask Him! As Jesus continued His teaching on prayer, He even tells us to ask for our daily bread (or provision)!

Do you remember the story of the blind beggar that cried out again and again for Jesus to have mercy on him? Jesus commanded the man to be brought to Him. The beggar knew what he wanted and needed. Everyone in the crowd knew what he wanted and needed. Jesus knew what he wanted and needed, yet He still asked the man, "**What do you want me to do for you?**" Why? Because it is important that we make our requests specific and clear (Luke 18:35–43).

Philippians 4:6 teaches us, "Be anxious for nothing, but in everything by prayer and supplication, with thanksgiving, let your requests be made known to God." The Greek word translated as *prayer* in that verse is a general term for "worship," but the word translated as *supplication* literally means "a detailed, specific request." Like the centurion, we should make our requests for healing unmistakably clear.

4. The humility in making the request

Great faith puts no confidence in good works or personal merit. The Jewish elders told Jesus that the centurion was deserving of having his request answered because "he loves our nation, and has built us a synagogue" (Luke 7:5).

But the centurion's opinion of himself was far different. He said that he was not worthy to have Jesus enter under his roof and that he didn't even think himself worthy to come to Jesus personally (Luke 7:6–7).

He had given a large sum of money to help God's work, maybe even to the point of personal sacrifice. He had taken an unpopular position as a supporter and even a champion of God's people in a time when they were not loved or looked upon with favor by Rome. He most certainly would have been ridiculed and perhaps even persecuted by his fellow Romans, but he looked to none of those things to somehow earn him favor with Jesus!

Some feel that because they have given to, served in, and even sacrificed for the church, they *deserve* to be healed or that somehow a miracle is due them. Not so, friend! We do not earn any blessings from God, healing included. What God does for us, He does by grace through faith so that no man can boast (Ephesians 2:8–9; Romans 4:16; 5:2; Galatians 3:5–6).

As long as we are looking to our good works, no matter how noble or numerous, we will always fall short. Salvation and all of the gifts that accompany it come freely by His hand of grace and they are received by the hand of faith.

Good works are the natural byproduct of a soul that has been changed by grace through faith. Good works are not the *root* of salvation; they are the *fruit* of salvation.

With the centurion, great humility preceded great faith. "God resists the proud, but gives grace to the humble" (James 4:6). Healing, like every blessing from heaven, comes to us on the wings of grace.

5. The faith behind the request

True faith is based upon the evidence of God's Word alone. His Word both creates and sustains faith. Jesus said that this Roman had great faith. As we look at this story, it is evident that the word of Jesus was central to the centurion's believing.

In Luke 7:7, he said to Jesus, "***Say the word, and my servant will be healed***." In essence, he said, "*All I need is your word. I don't need a feeling, a visible sign, or an angel to appear. Just speak the word!*" In Matthew's account he said, "*Only* speak a word" (Matthew 8:8). Great faith requires only the word of the Lord.

Great faith understands the authority of God's Word (v. 8). The centurion was saying, "My word makes things move and change and I know that Your Word will do the same. I speak and I know that my servant is carrying out what I commanded. I may not see him doing it, but I know it's being done. Jesus, You speak the word and even if I can't see anything, I know it's being done. If You speak to sickness to go, it will go. If You speak to healing to come, it will come!"

Spaghetti with Sausage and Peppers

My wife and I recently went out to dinner at a cozy little Italian restaurant near our house. We looked at the menu and I ordered spaghetti with sausage and peppers. The waitress wrote our order down and disappeared.

After she left, I didn't sit and wring my hands worrying over whether or not she had taken our order back to the kitchen. I didn't call the busboy over and ask him if he thought our food was being cooked.

When the waitress came back with our beverages, I didn't ask her, "Are you sure the cook is making our food? Did you see him making it?" I didn't think, *Maybe there's not even a cook back there!*

I didn't look at my wife and say, "What if they don't have any more ingredients? What if there are no more plates? What if the waitress falls and breaks her leg and the food never makes it to us? Why is it taking so long? I bet it's never coming!"

No! We didn't give it a thought. Once the word was spoken, we just sat and talked, enjoying each other's company as we drank our waters. As soon as I said, "Spaghetti with sausage and peppers," I counted it as done.

Friend, the word of the Lord has been spoken! By His stripes you were healed. Surely He has borne your sicknesses and carried your pains. He sent His Word and healed you and delivered you from that which destroys you.

The prayer of faith will heal the sick and the Lord will raise them up. His Word is life to the one who finds it and is health to all their flesh. He blesses our bread and water and takes sickness from our midst (Isaiah 53:4–5; 1 Peter 2:24; Psalm 107:20; James 5:14–15; Proverbs 4:20–22; Exodus 23:25).

God's Word is forever settled in heaven, but if it is going to benefit us on earth we must combine it with faith (Psalm 119:89; Hebrews 4:2). In the restaurant I considered it done and knew that my food would show up at the table, and it hadn't even been paid for yet!

Your healing and deliverance have already been paid for on the cross! Take Him at His Word, let your heart be at rest, and begin praising Him by faith. It's on the way, even if you can't see it. Great faith rests on the evidence of God's Word alone.

6. Jesus' willingness to answer the request

"Jesus went with them" (v. 6). There was no reluctance, no hesitation. He began moving toward the centurion even before He discovered his "great faith." Jesus hasn't changed. I believe that He begins moving toward us as soon as we lift our eyes to Him.

Trust Him. Look to Him. He is our compassionate High Priest who ever lives to make intercession for us (Hebrews 2:17; 7:25). Come boldly to the throne of grace to obtain mercy and to find grace to help in your time of need (Hebrews 4:14–16).

CHAPTER

6

A Funeral Interrupted

In four decades of pastoring, I have both officiated and attended more funerals than I care to remember. Some of those funerals were for people I didn't personally know and some were for people I was acquainted with, but the vast majority were held for people I knew well and loved deeply.

Out of all of those occasions, the most difficult were the ones where the parents were burying a child. Even though they knew that their child was in heaven, the grief at times was overwhelming.

As Dr. Luke continues his narrative, he now brings us to a story where there is grief upon grief. Not only has a parent lost a child, but he was an only child. Adding to the overwhelming sorrow of the event is the fact that this parent is also a widow. The poor woman we are going to read about has lost both her husband and her only son.

¹¹Now it happened, the day after, that He went into a city called Nain; and many of His disciples went with Him, and a large crowd. ¹²And when He came near the gate of the city, behold, a dead man was being carried out, the only son of his mother; and she was a widow. And a large crowd from the city was with her. ¹³When the Lord saw her, He had compassion on her and said to her, "Do not weep." ¹⁴Then He came and touched the open coffin, and those who carried him stood still. And He said, "Young man, I say to you, arise." ¹⁵So he who was dead sat up and began to speak. And He presented him to his mother. ¹⁶Then fear came upon all, and they glorified God, saying, "A great prophet has risen up among us"; and, "God has visited His people." ¹⁷And this report about Him went throughout all Judea and all the surrounding region. (Luke 7:11–17)

A Procession of Life Meets a Procession of Death

In this story there are two large crowds. One crowd is coming into the gates of the city of Nain while the other is passing out of those gates. The crowd moving down the narrow road entering the city is joyful with Jesus as the central figure.

The crowd that is leaving the city is sorrowful and full of grief with a dead boy being carried on a funeral bier as the central figure. One group represents life while the other represents death, and they are on a collision course. One will have to yield.

Jesus is the Prince and Author of life. Before Christ's resurrection, we are told that the devil had the power of death (Hebrews 2:14). Jesus is at the head of one procession while (figuratively speaking) the devil is at the head of the other. This story shows us in a graphic way that life is stronger than death and that Christ's power is far greater than that of the devil. Jesus came to destroy the works of the devil. The devil only comes to steal, to kill, and to destroy, but Jesus came to give us abundant life (1 John 3:8; John 10:10).

He Had Compassion on Her

The poor woman in this story was a widow. We are not told how long she had been without the companionship and support of her husband, but however long the duration, it would not have been an easy life for her in that time and culture. At least she had her son. He would have been the joy of her life, the single candle in her darkness, and if he were old enough, he was likely the one who now supported her. Then the unthinkable happened. Her son died. That flickering candle that brought light and joy to her home was suddenly and cruelly snuffed out. She was alone.

As ocean tides of grief rolled over her soul, no doubt many of the people of her small town sympathized with her and felt sorry for her. Perhaps a few mothers held their own sons a bit tighter that day as the sad and mournful procession slowly made its way from her home to the burial site outside of the city.

As they began to exit through the gates, something extraordinary happened. *Jesus saw her.* He saw her grief. He saw her broken heart and He understood. He knew she was alone. He knew the pain she was in now and He knew the pain that awaited her in her future. And *He had compassion on her.* He didn't feel compassion for the lad who had died. He was in paradise. He had compassion on *her.*

Jesus' compassion moved Him to action. It is something we see often in the life of Jesus.

Matthew 14:14 tells us, "When Jesus went out He *saw* a great multitude; and **He was moved with compassion** for them, and healed their sick" (emphasis mine).

On another occasion, as Jesus went out of Jericho, two blind men cried out to Him for mercy. Jesus called them over and asked what they wanted Him to do for them. After telling Him that they wanted their eyes to be opened, we are told, "***Jesus had compassion and touched their eyes***. And immediately their eyes received sight, and they followed Him" (Matthew 20:34, emphasis mine).

Another incident we read about tells us, "Now a leper came to Him, imploring Him, kneeling down to Him and saying to Him, 'If You are willing, You can make me clean.' Then ***Jesus, moved with compassion, stretched out His hand and touched him***, and said to him, 'I am willing; be cleansed.' As soon as He had spoken, immediately the leprosy left him, and he was cleansed" (Mark 1:40–42, emphasis mine).

It is important to remember that the Lord has not changed, nor will He. He is still full of compassion and He is touched deeply by our troubles. He is still the Healer, and we should have faith in His unfailing mercies. They are new every morning and His faithfulness is great (Lamentations 3:22–23; Hebrew 2:17; 4:15–16; 13:8; Psalm 103:1–5; 145:8–9).

His Love Has Been Poured Out in Our Hearts

The same love that His compassion springs from has been poured out into the heart of every believer (Romans 5:5). Generally, when the Lord brings healing, He does it through His people, the Church. As believers, we are commanded to lay our hands on the sick (Mark 16:18). God alone is the Healer, but we become the instruments He uses to bring about the healing.

We just listed several instances where Jesus was *moved* with compassion. When He followed that compassion, miracles occurred. When we are moved to action by the Lord's compassion that surfaces in our hearts, good things, sometimes even miraculous things, will follow.

An acquaintance of mine was speaking at a large crusade in South Africa. There was a poor woman who had been brought to the meeting who was totally paralyzed. She was lying on a mat, and several of the crusade speakers had prayed for her with no visible results. Standing next to her was her young child.

As the gentleman that I knew watched the scene unfold, a sudden compassion for the child came over him. He went and embraced the child and began to weep, almost uncontrollably. As he wept and cried out to God for the child, the power of God came upon the paralyzed mother and raised her up. She was instantly healed and stood to her feet. It was an electric moment in the meeting and the whole thing was captured on video.

The next time you sense God's compassion welling up within you, venture out. Offer to pray for the one that compassion is directed toward and remember that healing is God's business—we are just His vessels. I am convinced, however, that He is searching the body of Christ for those who will be willing and obedient to step out and be moved to action by compassion.

Second Corinthians 5:14 says, "The love of Christ compels us." Other translations say that it *urges* us, it *moves* us, and it *fuels our passion* and *motivates* us. As we move out and begin to follow the leading of His compassion, may great, God-glorifying miracles take place, and may it be said today as it was then, *God has visited His people.*

Before we move on to the next connected portion of this chapter concerning John the Baptist, here is a final thought.

In the Gospels, there are only three recorded occasions where Jesus raised someone from the dead, and in each case the people were young and tied in a unique way to their surviving family. Lazarus was young and he was the *only* brother of Mary and Martha. The daughter of

Jairus was only 12 years old and she was an *only* child. And here in Luke 7, the widow's *only* son whom Jesus raised from the dead was a young man (vv. 12, 14; John 11:1–44; Luke 8:41–55).

The Report Went Out

The report of the young man being raised from the dead at Nain went out throughout all Judea and all the surrounding region. It also made its way into the prison where John was being held (Luke 3:20; Matthew 11:2).

> ¹⁸Then the disciples of John reported to him concerning all these things. ¹⁹And John, calling two of his disciples to him, sent them to Jesus, saying, "Are You the Coming One, or do we look for another?" ²⁰When the men had come to Him, they said, "John the Baptist has sent us to You, saying, 'Are You the Coming One, or do we look for another?'" ²¹And that very hour He cured many of infirmities, afflictions, and evil spirits; and to many blind He gave sight. ²²Jesus answered and said to them, "Go and tell John the things you have seen and heard: that the blind see, the lame walk, the lepers are cleansed, the deaf hear, the dead are raised, the poor have the gospel preached to them. ²³And blessed is he who is not offended because of Me." (Luke 7:18–23)

Though having previously and publicly announced that Jesus was the promised Messiah, as he sat alone in that dark prison cell, John began to entertain some doubts. In order to settle the issue and put his mind and heart at rest, he sent directly to Jesus for an answer.

Interestingly enough, when Jesus talked to the multitudes after learning of John's doubts, He didn't criticize him or belittle him. He spoke highly of John and called him great (Luke 7:24–28). It's important to remember that a single failure or moment of weakness does not define us in the Lord's eyes. It is the entire journey that defines us, not a single event, whether it is positive or negative.

A Tree Is Known by Its Fruit

Jesus' answer to those whom John had sent was to continue in the work of healing and liberating those who were suffering. A tree is known by its fruit, and opening the eyes of the blind, unstopping the ears of the deaf, healing the lame and the sick, and preaching the gospel to the poor are all fruits that were to accompany the Messiah's ministry (Isaiah 35:3–6; 61:1).

The healing signs were all the proof Jesus would give to John as confirmation of His authenticity. There was no need to look for another, and the healings were proof of that. Is it possible that today some are *looking for another* because they haven't heard about or seen the supernatural?

Let us preach boldly to a hurting world that Jesus is the same yesterday, today, and forever and not be offended by what He is about! He is still healing sick bodies, delivering the oppressed, and reaching out to the poor with the good news, but He's doing it through His Church.

Why Don't We See More Healings?

> [18]For I will not dare to speak of any of those things which Christ has not accomplished through me, in word and deed, to make the Gentiles obedient—[19]in mighty signs and wonders, by the power of the Spirit of God, so that from Jerusalem and round about to Illyricum I have fully preached the gospel of Christ. (Romans 15:18–19)
>
> [4]And my speech and my preaching were not with persuasive words of human wisdom, but in demonstration of the Spirit

and of power, ⁵that your faith should not be in the wisdom of men but in the power of God. (1 Corinthians 2:4–5)

From the above verses it is evident that the apostle Paul considered supernatural demonstrations of the Holy Spirit to be an integral part of preaching the gospel. And to any open-hearted person today, one does not have to go far or look for too long to hear of or to see the Holy Spirit at work, especially in the arena of healing.

But I will be the first to admit that the infrequency of seeing and experiencing His healing hand at work is troubling, to say the least. It's not that it hasn't happened or isn't happening. It is. I just think we should be seeing more of it.

Following are two reasons why I believe we don't see divine healings take place more often, and once we realize the *why*, we can see a clear pathway to open a possible floodgate of the supernatural.

1. Unbelief

In Mark's Gospel, we are told of when Jesus returned to His hometown and began teaching in the local synagogue. It says:

> ¹Then He went out from there and came to His own country, and His disciples followed Him. ²And when the Sabbath had come, He began to teach in the synagogue. And many hearing Him were astonished, saying, "Where did this Man get these things? And what wisdom is this which is given to Him, that such mighty works are performed by His hands! ³Is this not the carpenter, the Son of Mary, and brother of James, Joses, Judas, and Simon? And are not His sisters here with us?" So they were offended at Him.

⁴But Jesus said to them, "A prophet is not without honor except in his own country, among his own relatives, and in his own house." ⁵Now He could do no mighty work there, except that He laid His hands on a few sick people and healed them. ⁶And He marveled because of their unbelief. Then He went about the villages in a circuit, teaching. (Mark 6:1–6)

Did you notice that in verse 5 it said He could do no mighty work there? Not that He *wouldn't*, He *couldn't*! He was only able to heal a few "sickly" (literal Greek) people, but He could perform no mighty work of healing, no miracle.

In the NLT translation, Mark 6:5 reads, "And because of their unbelief, he couldn't do any miracles among them except to place his hands on a few sick people and heal them."

The people of His home village refused to honor Him, and because of community unbelief they limited what He could do among them. In fact, Jesus marveled at their unbelief! If unbelief could limit and hinder healing and miracles then, it can do the same now!

If you think about it, there are entire churches and denominations that not only do not teach on healing, they teach and warn people against it! With that in mind, is it any wonder why we do not see as much healing today as we would like?

The answer to that, and a major way to turn the tide so that we see more healings take place, is to teach and preach on it. That was Jesus' response to their unbelief. He went about the villages in a circuit, teaching (v. 6).

"Faith comes by hearing, and hearing by the word of God." (Romans 10:17) "Does God give you the Spirit because you follow the law? Does God work miracles among you because you follow the law? No,

God gives you His Spirit and works miracles among you because you heard the message about Jesus and believed it" (Galatians 3:5 ERV).

2. Desire

In 1 Corinthians 12, the apostle Paul gives us the definitions of the nine gifts of the Spirit. Among them are the working of miracles, the gifts of healings, special faith, the word of knowledge, the word of wisdom, and the discerning of spirits, as well as the utterance gifts of tongues, the interpretation of tongues, and prophecy.

In chapter 13, Paul deals with the spirit that should characterize their use—love. And in chapter 14, he talks about their proper use in the local church.

It is very illuminating to note the language the apostle uses when he speaks of their use and manifestation among the believers in that fourteenth chapter. He told them to *desire* spiritual gifts, to *earnestly desire* the best gifts, to be *zealous* for spiritual gifts and to *seek to excel* in spiritual gifts. All of that language speaks of desire and spiritual hunger.

The gifts of the Spirit do not manifest because we are mature or because we have walked with the Lord for many years. They manifest because we are earnestly seeking God for them! **They work by desire, not by maturity!**

And yes, we understand they work as the Spirit wills, not as we will, but I am convinced that He is much more willing than we have been. He has and will continue to meet us at the level of our desire. Make seeking the manifestations of the Spirit, including the working of miracles and the gifts of healings, a regular part of your daily prayer. Pray that we will see them in manifestation in our churches and as we go out and mingle among the lost and needy people of this world. I believe that as we do, the Holy Spirit won't be long in meeting us.

CHAPTER

7

Healed of Evil Spirits and Infirmities

Years ago, an old missionary I knew shared how in the 1950s he was ministering in a major city in China. God had put it on his heart to go into Tibet, but he had no funds to do so. One evening as he preached to the small group of people that had gathered, several men brought a woman into the meeting on a bed. It was easy to see that she was a woman of wealth due to her clothing and because of those who attended to her.

She was carried in on the bed because of a serious physical condition and was scheduled to have a major surgery the following week to try and correct the condition. Someone had told her about the small gatherings where an American missionary was preaching and praying for the sick. She decided to come. After listening to the message, she asked for prayer. She was healed and walked out under her own power.

The next day several men arrived where the missionary was staying. They brought baskets of delicious food and a large sum of money.

They said that the lady who was healed had sent them with the gifts. She said, "This is the same amount of money that I would have had to spend on the operation. Please use it to carry on the Lord's work." It was all the money and supplies necessary for the trip into Tibet, which was undertaken just a few days afterward.

As we continue reading Luke's account of Jesus' healing ministry, we find an anecdote about several women who were not dissimilar to the Chinese woman who supported the work of the American missionary.

> [1]Now it came to pass, afterward, that He went through every city and village, preaching and bringing the glad tidings of the kingdom of God. And the twelve were with Him, [2]and certain women who had been healed of evil spirits and infirmities—Mary called Magdalene, out of whom had come seven demons, [3]and Joanna the wife of Chuza, Herod's steward, and Susanna, and many others who provided for Him from their substance. (Luke 8:1–3)

Three women are mentioned here by name: Mary Magdalene (whom we find at the crucifixion, burial, and resurrection of Jesus), Joanna, and Susanna. The final two are mentioned nowhere else in Scripture. These three, along with *many other* women, provided for and supported Jesus and the Twelve with their own money and resources.

All of these women had at least two things in common: first, they had been healed or set free by Jesus from sicknesses and evil spirits, and secondly, they all supported Him and His disciples out of their personal funds.

Gratitude—Not Obligation

Was Mary Magdalene trying to repay Jesus for casting the seven demons out of her? Were these other women trying to pay for their healing or deliverance? No. Miracles are not for sale. The women gave out of gratitude and out of a desire to see others receive what they had received. They supported His ministry with grateful hearts, not out of a begrudging obligation.

In Luke 12:34, Jesus said, "***For where your treasure is, there your heart will be also***." Their hearts were with Jesus, so their resources were there also. It is an inescapable truth that *we invest in what we love and value*. If someone claims to love God and His work but they give nothing or very little to His kingdom, they are either lying or are self-deceived.

Imagine what torments Mary Magdalene went through when she had seven evil spirits afflicting her. No rest, plagued by unclean and depressing thoughts—day by day it must have seemed like the life was being squeezed out of her.

And then suddenly, by a word or a touch from the Master, she is free! Her mind is clear. The agony of a dark uncleanness and depressing evil has not just abated, it has gone! Oh, the tears she must have shed. The joy, gratitude, and reverence that now filled her heart. There is nothing she wouldn't do or give for the Savior.

At the same time, a great compassion for others suffering under the heel of Satan must have laid hold of her heart. They could be set free too. Mary knew the depths of despair and the utter hopelessness caused by the demon powers that had seized her, and she also knew the One with the greater authority and the compassion to set people free. Out of that knowledge, and with thankful hearts, Mary, along with these other women, supported the work of Christ.

All of the Money in the World

Being healed or set free by Jesus ought to help anyone have a right perspective on money. All of the money in the world won't help you if you're plagued by a demon, nor will it substitute for lost health.

A friend and I were talking in my backyard one day. He has been extremely successful in business, but at that time his child was having some severe psychological problems. I will never forget what he said to me through tears: "I would give everything I have if my son could just be normal." That is the heart of every good parent. There is nothing we would not give to see our children or loved ones healed and whole.

Even as we consider how God, through the sacrifice of Christ, has delivered us from sin and from an eternity of torment in hell, how can we not freely offer to Him our all? With grateful hearts we should happily support the work of Jesus in the world today. As we tithe and give to our local church, we enable them to continue the good work of soul winning and making disciples, and as we generously give to global missions, which normally are connected to the local church, we become co-laborers with those who are sent out to share the good news with those we can't personally reach.

Part of Your Life

When a person works at their job, as well as laboring to create something that will be helpful or meet a particular need, they are, in essence, trading part of their life for a paycheck. If I get paid every two weeks, then the sixty, eighty, or ninety hours I worked during those two weeks is traded for an agreed upon sum. My paycheck literally represents the portion of my life that I traded for it.

When I choose to give a portion of that check to God's work out of a grateful and obedient heart, quite literally, I am giving that portion of my time and life that I traded for that money. That is a sacred thing and should never be treated lightly.

If, for some reason, you do not tithe and give generously to the work of Christ, perhaps it is time to examine your heart.

What do you love more than God that you invest in? Do you only give God and His work your leftovers? Is He not worth more than that? Have you left your first love? Have you been hurt by someone or by something that happened in a church? Whatever the reason, get it sorted out, and together, let us through our praying, giving, and going continue to bring a living Jesus to a dying world.

Storms, Demons, Swine, and the Great Things God Has Done

Though Luke does not give us much information about Mary Magdalene's deliverance from seven evil spirits, the next case he shares with us is rich with both drama and detail. It begins with a storm.

> 22Now it happened, on a certain day, that He got into a boat with His disciples. And He said to them, "Let us cross over to the other side of the lake." And they launched out. 23But as they sailed He fell asleep. And a windstorm came down on the lake, and they were filling with water, and were in jeopardy. 24And they came to Him and awoke Him, saying, "Master, Master, we are perishing!"
>
> Then He arose and rebuked the wind and the raging of the water. And they ceased, and there was a calm. 25But He said to them, "Where is your faith?"
>
> And they were afraid, and marveled, saying to one another, "Who can this be? For He commands even the winds and water, and they obey Him!"

²⁶Then they sailed to the country of the Gadarenes, which is opposite Galilee. ²⁷And when He stepped out on the land, there met Him a certain man from the city who had demons for a long time. And he wore no clothes, nor did he live in a house but in the tombs. ²⁸When he saw Jesus, he cried out, fell down before Him, and with a loud voice said, "What have I to do with You, Jesus, Son of the Most High God? I beg You, do not torment me!" ²⁹For He had commanded the unclean spirit to come out of the man. For it had often seized him, and he was kept under guard, bound with chains and shackles; and he broke the bonds and was driven by the demon into the wilderness.

³⁰Jesus asked him, saying, "What is your name?"

And he said, "Legion," because many demons had entered him. ³¹And they begged Him that He would not command them to go out into the abyss.

³²Now a herd of many swine was feeding there on the mountain. So they begged Him that He would permit them to enter them. And He permitted them. ³³Then the demons went out of the man and entered the swine, and the herd ran violently down the steep place into the lake and drowned.

³⁴When those who fed them saw what had happened, they fled and told it in the city and in the country. ³⁵Then they went out to see what had happened, and came to Jesus, and found the man from whom the demons had departed, sitting at the feet of Jesus, clothed and in his right mind. And they were afraid. ³⁶They also who had seen it told them by what means he who had been demon-possessed

was healed. ³⁷Then the whole multitude of the surrounding region of the Gadarenes asked Him to depart from them, for they were seized with great fear. And He got into the boat and returned.

³⁸Now the man from whom the demons had departed begged Him that he might be with Him. (Luke 8:22–38)

This journey across the water began with Jesus saying to His disciples, "Let us cross over to the other side of the lake." He didn't just say that He was going to cross over, He said, "Let us cross over." He didn't say, "Let us go halfway across and sink," or "Let us go halfway across and if a storm comes, let's turn back." He said they were going to cross over. His word should have been enough for them, storm or no storm. In fact, the storm didn't disturb Him, but the unbelief of His disciples did. May we learn to confidently rely on His Word, regardless of the obstacles or troubles we face.

No Accident

The only thing that Jesus did once they got to the other side of the lake was to set the demoniac free. Consider how far Jesus came, the cost, the inconvenience, the time, the opposition of the storm . . . all to set one person free. God may be extravagant, but He is never wasteful. He will go to great lengths just to reach and rescue one person.

And rest assured, this storm that opposed them and threatened to sink them was no accident. It was not just something that randomly happened. I believe that Jesus was being directed by the Father to a soul that was crying out in torment for help. That is why He determined to cross the lake at that time. If we looked behind the curtain of the natural, we would see Satan stirring up this storm to try and stop Jesus.

From reading the book of Job, we can see clearly that Satan can affect the natural elements. He caused a great wind that collapsed a house, killing all of Job's children.

After the disciples awoke Jesus, He arose and *rebuked* the wind. It is the identical word used in Luke 4:35 where Jesus *rebuked* a demon. In fact, when Jesus rebuked the demon, He said, "*Be still*" (or quite literally, "*Be muzzled*") and come out of him," which according to Mark's account of this encounter with the storm is the exact phrase that Jesus used on the wind: "*Be still (muzzled)!*" (Mark 4:39 AMPC). Jesus treated the storm as if it were something from the hand of the enemy, not from God's hand!

For those who are actively engaged in Kingdom enterprise, there is no doubt that many of the storms and troubles that come into our own lives come for the same reason. We are on a mission from God to reach sighing, crying, dying humanity with the gospel, and we can't let the storms of life stop us or distract us from our destination.

Out of the Man and into the Pigs

Once Jesus reached the opposite shore, He cast the demons out of the man, and with His permission, they entered a herd of swine, which numbered about two thousand according to Mark's account. The swine immediately ran down a steep place and were drowned in the lake. Once news got out about what had happened, a multitude from that region came and asked Jesus to depart from them.

Jesus sacrificed 2,000 swine in the process of delivering one man, and by so doing gives us something of God's perspective as to the value of a person. Those pigs were worth a huge sum of money, but Jesus thought that the man was worth more. Wherever Christianity comes, it brings a supreme respect for the value of people.

Where Christianity is suppressed, man becomes of little more value than a beast in the eyes of tyrants, a cog in the machine to be worn and worked for the good of the machine, a number on a list of another's selfish calculations . . . something cheap and expendable.

That's the way these men of Gadara viewed life. They were willing to deal in a trade that was forbidden by Jewish law in order to make their fortunes by selling to the Romans, who would have bought and eaten the swine. They begged Christ to go and leave them to their pig breeding. They had the Son of God with them, but they preferred swine!

The Gadarenes are still about today. They aren't necessarily hostile to the faith, but if they are to entertain it, it must not interfere with their lives or cost them anything. But the gospel does disrupt. It changes everything. It sets a higher value on the souls of men than on material possessions. It always compels us to look at life through different eyes.

The presence of Jesus healed men, but it was irrelevant to these men if swine were lost. This region of ten towns called Decapolis was willing to sell their place in history for pork!

Return and Tell

The man who had been set free, though wanting to stay with Jesus, was told by the Lord to "***Return to your own house and tell what great things God has done for you***" (Luke 8:39). It was in the harsh environment where Jesus had just been asked to leave where this man was left to tell his story.

I have had numerous people throughout the years ask me to pray that they can get a job where they aren't surrounded by sinners, or that they can move into an apartment complex where they will be surrounded by Christians. I never pray with them for those things.

Instead, I always encourage them to look for opportunities to share their faith. "God has you there to be a witness," I tell them. "You are salt and light. Light in their darkness, an oasis in their desert, and a preserving agent where there is decay. Stay right where you are and let God use you."

Every believer needs to be telling others about the great things that God has done for them. Some have been delivered from drugs, some from depression, others from demons, deviant behavior, or disease. And all of God's children have been delivered from the eternal consequence of sin. Everyone who names the name of Christ has a story to tell!

He Began to Proclaim in Decapolis

Luke tells us that the man obediently went his way and proclaimed throughout the whole city what great things Jesus had done for him (Luke 8:39). But as we stitch the other Gospel narratives to Luke's story, we get a fuller picture of what happened. Mark tells us that the man didn't stop with his own city. His account says, he ***"began to proclaim in Decapolis** all that Jesus had done for him, and all marveled"* (Mark 5:20). Decapolis was a region consisting of ten towns.

In Mark 7:31, we read that Jesus once again "came through the midst of the region of Decapolis." Matthew's parallel account to this tells us that at that time "great multitudes came to Him, having with them the lame, blind, mute, maimed, and many others; and they laid them down at Jesus' feet, and He healed them. So the multitude marveled when they saw the mute speaking, the maimed made whole, the lame walking, and the blind seeing; and they glorified the God of Israel" (Matthew 15:30–31).

This is remarkable. The people of that region have shifted from being fearful and begging Jesus to leave them to bringing their sick to Him and laying them at His feet! What brought about this dramatic change? The testimony of the man that had been set free from demon powers by Jesus! Psalm 105:1 says, "Make known His deeds among the peoples!" Don't underestimate the power of your testimony.

When I was in Bible school, the couple living in the apartment next to mine were also students. One night outside of a Denny's restaurant, they prayed for a man with a cane who was struggling to walk. He was instantly and wonderfully healed. They asked him if he would share his story, to which he gladly agreed. They then marched up and down the block, stopping every person they ran into and had the man share the story of what just happened. After he told his story, they would ask the people if they wanted to put their trust in Jesus. Person after person bowed their head and prayed the sinner's prayer, accepting Jesus into their hearts.

What is your Decapolis? What might God do in the lives of those who hear your story? Be proactive about sharing the good things that God has done in your life. If He has answered prayers, tell someone. If He has healed you, shout it from the rooftops. If He has given you peace, someone in your world needs to hear that. If you have known the grace and mercy of His forgiveness, share it because someone needs to hear it, and you never know how great a gospel fire might be kindled by your little spark.

Not Under a Microscope

It is interesting that Dr. Luke begins chapter 8 by saying that Jesus healed people of *evil spirits and infirmities* (v. 2). In so doing, he is acknowledging that the source of some illnesses and conditions could be directly attributed to the presence of an evil spirit. There are evil spirits that cause and then enforce illness, and that is something that could not be found under a microscope!

In chapter 13, Luke even speaks of a woman who had a *spirit of infirmity* for eighteen years. Today, her condition may have been labeled a number of different ways, but the trained physician, Dr. Luke, went right to the source and called it for what it was.

In today's world of modern science, what would they have said about the demoniac that lived among the tombs? They might have been able to sedate him, but they could not have cured him because his problem was spiritual—he was possessed by evil spirits!

How he came to such a state, we are not told. Perhaps it began because he was dabbling in the occult, or maybe he began to slowly yield his will to an evil spirit as it seduced and tempted him again and again until finally, he was mastered by it. However it happened, he was in the sorriest of states.

Think of his condition. He had demons in him *for a long time* (Luke 8:27). According to Mark's account, he had *often* been hunted and captured and chained only to break free and escape (Mark 5:4). If we look closely at Luke's account in chapter 8, as well as those in the other Gospels, we can see six expressions of the work of these evil spirits in his life:

1. **He was isolated.** The demon had driven him into the wilderness (v. 29). The devil always wants to isolate people. That is when we are most vulnerable.

2. **He was unclean**. He was both morally and physically unclean. He wore no clothes and he lived among the tombs (v. 27).

3. **He had no restraint.** He was not restrained by the laws of God or by the chains of men.

4. **He was restless.** He cried out night and day (Mark 5:5).

5. **He harmed himself.** He didn't just show a lack of care for his body, he purposely harmed it, cutting himself with stones (Mark 5:5).

6. **He was a danger and a menace to others.** He was exceedingly fierce, so that no one could pass that way (Matthew 8:28).

Jesus set the man free, and the results were tangible and immediate. He was no longer isolated. He was no longer unclean or restless. When the men of that region arrived, they found him clothed, sitting at the feet of Jesus, and in his right mind (v. 35).

Did this man previously have a wife and family? Perhaps, for Jesus told him to *return to his own house* and tell people what God had done for him (Luke 8:39). In Mark's account, Jesus said, "*Go home to your friends.*" What a reunion that must have been! Blessed Savior who delivers us in our spirits, minds, and bodies!

CHAPTER

8

Twelve Years of Sunshine and Twelve Years of Suffering

As we continue on in Luke's account of Jesus' healing ministry, we come to two stories that cross paths and intertwine with each other. One is about a couple's only child who lay dying and the other is about a woman who had hemorrhaged for many years without relief. In them, we find some amazing insights into divine healing and how it may be procured.

As the story opens up, we find Jesus and His ministry gladly welcomed by the Galileans after He was rejected by the Gadarenes. Into this crowd of eager people came someone they all knew—a man named Jairus, a ruler from their local synagogue . . . and he was desperate.

> [40]So it was, when Jesus returned, that the multitude welcomed Him, for they were all waiting for Him. [41]And behold, there came a man named Jairus, and he was a ruler of the synagogue. And he fell down at Jesus' feet and begged Him to come to his house, [42]for he had an only daughter about

twelve years of age, and she was dying. But as He went, the multitudes thronged Him. (Luke 8:40–42)

He Fell at His Feet

Luke paints a graphic picture of what happened. When Jairus reached Jesus, he didn't demand anything or put in a polite request for assistance. He fell at Jesus' feet and begged. Matthew 9:18 tells us that when he arrived, he "worshiped" Jesus. The Greek word translated there as *worship* literally means "to lie prostrate before and venerate." There was nothing dignified about it. It was the desperate action of a man who was looking to Jesus as his only hope.

Think of it: Jairus was a ruler of the synagogue, a spiritual leader in the community. If you had marriage problems, you went to Jairus for answers. If you had questions about the Scriptures or needed guidance, you went to Jairus for help. And here he is, humbling himself before everyone, lying in the dirt before Jesus, willing to admit that he doesn't have all the answers and that he is in need.

This ruler came to the right place to find healing for his daughter—the feet of Jesus. It is an amazing study if you look through the Gospels and see how many people found wholeness at His feet. It is the place to which we must all come when seeking help and healing, but pride keeps many from getting there.

Jairus could have thought, *I can't lie at His feet in front of everyone. What will they think? What will they say? A lot of my colleagues don't like Jesus.* He put any such thoughts aside and came to Jesus with absolute humility, lying before the Lord to make his petition regardless of what anyone else thought or said.

Many years ago on a Sunday morning, I was teaching on the healing of blind Bartimaeus and how he cried out more and more for mercy from Jesus, even though people were telling him to be quiet. It is a Sunday I never shall forget. At the end of the sermon, a respected businessman in our church fell to his knees and began to loudly cry out to God for mercy.

I knew the man personally and was aware of a debilitating physical condition that he had. He wore a substantial back brace due to extreme back pain. His range of motion was limited, and I had seen him on several occasions wince in pain when he moved, even slightly, in the wrong way.

That morning he humbled himself before family and friends as he repeatedly cried out for mercy. After several minutes, he became quiet, got off of his knees, and sat down again. He had been miraculously healed. He summarily discarded the back brace, and I can personally testify to his healing as we enjoyed several games of golf together. He was never troubled with the same condition again.

Jesus Went with Him

One of the things that stands out to me is that without any seeming hesitation, Jesus went with Jairus to heal his daughter. When a request was made to heal Peter's mother-in-law, Jesus responded without delay. The Lord did not turn away any who came to Him for healing at the door of Peter's house in Capernaum, nor did He refuse the leper who came for healing. When the multitudes came to hear and be healed, there is no record of any being turned away empty—all were healed. And just as He does here for Jairus, He came for the centurion's servant when requested (Luke 4:38–40; 5:12–15; 6:17–19; 7:1–6).

Let us take the time to deeply consider the Lord's willingness to heal. To see Jesus is to see the Father. He is the will of God in action. As we read through Luke, as well as the other Gospels, we find that healing was a very high priority for Jesus. He spent so much time healing, as we read it almost seems as though *He has just come from healing someone, is in the process of healing someone, or is going to heal someone.*

Dear friend, He has not changed. His will has not changed. Read the stories. Linger there. Dare to let hope arise in your heart, for faith gives substance to things hoped for.

A Sudden Interruption

> [43]Now a woman, having a flow of blood for twelve years, who had spent all her livelihood on physicians and could not be healed by any, [44]came from behind and touched the border of His garment. And immediately her flow of blood stopped. [45]And Jesus said, "Who touched Me?" When all denied it, Peter and those with him said, "Master, the multitudes throng and press You, and You say, 'Who touched Me?'" [46]But Jesus said, "Somebody touched Me, for I perceived power going out from Me." [47]Now when the woman saw that she was not hidden, she came trembling; and falling down before Him, she declared to Him in the presence of all the people the reason she had touched Him and how she was healed immediately. [48]And He said to her, "Daughter, be of good cheer; your faith has made you well. Go in peace." (Luke 8:43–48)

As they were proceeding to the ruler's house, there was a sudden interruption that stopped everything. A woman came from behind, touched the hem of His garment, and was healed. Jesus stopped the whole procession to discover who had done this and to speak encouraging words to them.

Luke tells us that she spent everything she had on physicians, yet none of them could heal her. Mark adds that *"she had suffered many*

things from many physicians and rather than getting better, ***she grew worse*** (Mark 5:25–26). Apparently they experimented on her or subjected her to many painful or unnecessary treatments. It was all unfruitful. Instead of the sickness disappearing, the only thing that disappeared was all of her money.

Jesus did not initiate her healing, she did. It was not a sovereign act of God. In fact, Jesus turned to the crowd and asked, "Who touched Me?" The disciples pointed out that many had been touching Him, as the crowd had been pressing up against Him and thronging Him (v. 45). In fact, the Greek word translated *throng* literally means "to press up against so hard as to almost strangle or suffocate."

Some had touched Him, no doubt, from being inadvertently pushed into Him by the surge of the crowd. Others may have touched Him out of curiosity, hoping something might happen. Some did so, perhaps, just because He was famous. But of all the touches that day, only one arrested His attention. It was the touch of faith.

Jesus perceived that healing power had gone out of Him into someone. He hadn't planned on it happening, but He knew immediately when it did (v. 46). Mark 5:32 says, "He looked around to see her who had done this thing." "*This thing*" did not refer to the mere act of being touched, for many had done that. "This thing" was to draw healing power out of Him. She had done it through her faith.

As well as calling her "Daughter" and telling her to "be of good cheer," Jesus specifically declared that her faith had made her well. Jesus can still be touched by faith today.

Trust in the Promises

We trust in the Lord by trusting in His promises. Faith in His Word is faith in Him. Luke specifically tells us that this woman touched (literally *clutched* or *grasped*—there was nothing tentative about it) the border or hem of His garment.

Why did she do that? Why did she say, "If only I may touch His garment, I shall be made well" (Matthew 9:21)?

The answer is very likely tied up in a promise. In the last chapter of the last book of the Old Testament, there is a prophecy about the coming Messiah. It declares, He "shall arise with healing in His wings" (Malachi 4:2). The word for *wings* is the same word for "the hem or border of a garment" (Numbers 15:38; 1 Samuel 24:4). With a fair degree of certainty, we can say that this woman was acting on God's promise given through Malachi. Her faith was anchored in God's Word.

If She Can Be Healed by Her Faith, I Can Be Healed by Mine

I have always loved this story about the woman who was healed from her twelve-year-long flow of blood and I have preached many sermons based on it. I will never forget one evening in particular back in the early 1980s when I was doing just that.

A faithful member of our church brought a friend of hers to the service to hear the message. Her friend was a believer, but she had never heard a sermon on the subject of healing. She also happened to be suffering from several serious maladies.

At the close of the service, she came forward for prayer with a piece of paper in her hand. "*I have made a list of everything I need to be healed from. If that woman with the flow of blood could be healed by her faith, I can be healed by mine! I believe that Jesus is going to heal me when we pray,*" she boldly declared. There were several things on the list, but two stood out to me: a heart condition and hereditary diabetes. We prayed together for her healing, after which she lifted her hands as she began praising God.

The next day she called the office and asked if she could come in and speak with me. I had an opening in my schedule, so I accommodated her. When she came in she was ecstatic! "I am healed!"

She told me, "My grandfather died of diabetes. His feet began to bleed. They amputated toes and eventually his feet. It continued to progress until he died from it. The same thing happened to my dad. For several years now, I have had open sores between my toes that will not heal—they bleed continually. Every night, my stockings are full of blood when I pull them off. But last night, after I got home from church I was not bleeding! I even pulled my toes apart with force to try and make them bleed, but they wouldn't bleed! I'm healed and I know that when I go to the doctor he's going to tell me that my heart is normal too!" When she did finally see a doctor about her heart, it was confirmed that God had healed that too.

Jairus Has Been Waiting

While this whole scene with the woman healed of the flow of blood unfolded, Jairus has been waiting. In his mind, every moment would have been critical, yet Jesus has stopped the procession to find out who touched Him and then to talk to them!

Little does Jairus know that the words Jesus spoke to the woman in verse 48, "*Your faith has made you well*," would be spoken to him almost verbatim in just a few moments. And seeing the display of healing power coupled with the Lord's tenderness to the woman would be more important than Jairus could have ever realized because he is about to get the worst news that his ears have ever heard.

> [49]While He was still speaking, someone came from the ruler of the synagogue's house, saying to him, "Your daughter is dead. Do not trouble the Teacher." [50]But when Jesus heard

it, He answered him, saying, "Do not be afraid; only believe, and she will be made well." (Luke 8:49–50)

Jairus had just witnessed the healing of the woman who had been hemorrhaging for twelve years. Jesus had said to her, "*Your faith (or believing) has made you well.*"

Now Jesus says to him, "*Only believe (and your daughter) will be made well.*"

As soon as Jesus heard the report being told to Jairus that his daughter was dead, He told him to **not do** something and to **do** something. He told him to not fear and instead to only believe. To *only* believe means that you entertain no doubts.

Doubts and fears may come knocking at the door and we can't stop that from happening, but we do not have to *entertain* them and think on them. To be successful in doing that, we must focus on what the Lord has said about our situation. In the case of Jairus, it was that his daughter would be made well.

Proverbs 4:20–22 says,

> [20]My son, give attention to my words; incline your ear to my sayings. [21]Do not let them depart from your eyes; keep them in the midst of your heart; [22]for they are life to those who find them, and health to all their flesh.

That is great advice for anyone seeking healing and, in essence, it is what Jairus needed to do. When our attention is focused upon the promises, there is no room for doubt or fear. Faith comes from hearing the Word and it is sustained as we continue to give our attention to that Word. When faith fills the heart, it dispels fear.

He Put Them All Outside

> ⁵¹When He came into the house, He permitted no one to go in except Peter, James, and John, and the father and mother of the girl. ⁵²Now all wept and mourned for her; but He said, "Do not weep; she is not dead, but sleeping." ⁵³And they ridiculed Him, knowing that she was dead. ⁵⁴But He put them all outside, took her by the hand and called, saying, "Little girl, arise." (Luke 8:51–54)

Jesus was very selective as to who He allowed to go into the room where the little girl's body lay. He only had His inner circle of Peter, James, and John, along with the girl's parents go in with Him.

In fact, when it came to the mourners turned ridiculers, He actually put them all outside. The phrase, *"He put them all outside"* (also found in Mark 5:40 and Matthew 9:25), is not gentle in any sense. It literally means "He threw them out."

There is an important lesson for us in what Jesus did on this occasion. Jesus had told Jairus to *only believe* right before they got to the house where the atmosphere would be heavy with the ridicule and unbelief of the gathered crowd. He separated that crowd from Jairus . . . forcefully.

When we find ourselves in critical situations or believing for the restoration of our health, as much as possible, it is imperative that we separate ourselves from the doubt peddlers and mockers.

In writing to the Galatian church, Paul made it clear that the Christians there had allowed the unbelief and wrong thinking of others to affect their faith (Galatians 3:1; 5:7–9). Whenever we are in a battle, it is always good to surround ourselves with people of like precious faith who will stand with us and encourage us rather than drag us down.

Don't Let Anyone in Who Doesn't Have Faith in God

Years ago I was attending a meeting where the son-in-law of a famous missionary to South Africa was speaking. He shared this story about his father-in-law: it was the early 1900s and there wasn't much available when it came to medical care in the region where they labored. One day a terrible accident happened to the missionary's wife. Her life was in jeopardy, and even if proper medical treatment had been available, she may not have survived. They laid her on a bed and began to pray, but before they began, his father-in-law stationed a large woman at the front door with the explicit instructions to *not let anyone through that door who doesn't have faith in God.*

While she barred the way of the curious and even the concerned, they continued to kneel by the wife's bedside and pray. After several hours she stood to her feet, healed, and finished her household chores before retiring to bed.

> [54]But He put them all outside, took her by the hand and called, saying, "Little girl, arise." [55]Then her spirit returned, and she arose immediately. And He commanded that she be given something to eat. [56]And her parents were astonished, but He charged them to tell no one what had happened. (Luke 8:54–56)

After putting the people outside, Jesus spoke to the little girl. He spoke as if she could hear Him, and she did. She had not ceased to exist. She (her spirit) had just left her body, which the Bible calls death (James 2:26).

Upon hearing the voice of her Creator, her spirit returned (Colossians 1:15–17). Then Jesus commanded that she be given something to eat. It was necessary for her to recover her strength. Even when God miraculously intervenes and brings healing or restoration, we still must exercise common sense, caring for and nourishing our bodies with proper food if we are to maintain our health.

He Responds to Faith

As we reflect upon this wonderful, intertwined story of the woman who was healed from hemorrhaging and the daughter of Jairus who was brought back to life, several things stand out.

The daughter of Jairus was twelve years old. Their family had enjoyed twelve years of sunshine, twelve years of delight and happiness, when she was suddenly struck down. The woman with the issue of blood had endured twelve years of suffering. She had experienced twelve years of darkness where she was treated as a social outcast. For twelve years she had known pain, loneliness, and lack.

It's not that God had some sort of balance in His hand, saying, "*Okay, woman that's hemorrhaging, you've suffered enough. And Jairus, you've had twelve blessed years, so now it's your turn.*"

There was and is no such thinking or dealings from God. These stories are not about God somehow leveling the scale when it comes to human suffering. They are about the Lord's willingness to heal and how He responds to faith.

And our faith need not be perfect before God will intervene. In Luke 7:9, Jesus declared that the Roman centurion had great faith for saying *Jesus need not come* (but to only speak the word). Jairus said, "*I want you to come to my house.*" The woman said, "*I'll go to you.*"

All of them had different expressions of faith, some more mature than others, some in need of encouragement to not be afraid, but all were responded to by Jesus. Wherever you are in your journey of faith, remember, He is the same compassionate Lord today as He was then. Trust Him.

CHAPTER

9

Called, Given, and Sent

¹Then He called His twelve disciples together and gave them power and authority over all demons, and to cure diseases. ²He sent them to preach the kingdom of God and to heal the sick.... ⁶So they departed and went through the towns, preaching the gospel and healing everywhere. (Luke 9:1–2, 6)

As we begin reading in Luke 9, immediately we are met with an occurrence of great significance. For the first time, Jesus sends out others to represent Him. The Twelve are sent on their first mission and healing the sick is a big part of it. In fact, we find that three things were done by the Lord in connection with the Twelve going out to preach and to heal. He *called* them, He *gave* to them, and He *sent* them.

Called

First, He called them. That not only denotes a sacred commission to go and represent Him, but it was first a calling *to be with Him*. In Mark's account of these things we read, "Then He appointed twelve, *that they might be with Him* and that He might send them out to preach, and to have power to heal sicknesses and to cast out demons" (Mark 3:14–15, emphasis mine).

They were called to be with Him before they were sent out to represent Him. The lesson is clear. If we are to have any success as His representatives, if our preaching and ministering to the sick or demonized is going to bear any lasting fruit, we must first be with Him.

He is our source. He is the author and finisher of our faith, and without Him we can do nothing. Time spent at His feet, worshiping and drinking in His words is never wasted. It is, in fact, vital to any fruitful ministry. As believers today, we are called to preach the gospel and to lay hands on the sick to bring healing, but first, we have been called into the fellowship of His Son (Hebrews 12:2; John 15:5; Mark 16:15–18; 1 Corinthians 1:9; 1 John 1:3).

After the lame man was healed at the gate of the temple, Peter spoke boldly to the rulers, elders, scribes, and the high priest. Then we read, "Now when they saw the boldness of Peter and John, and perceived that they were uneducated and untrained men, they marveled. And *they realized that they had been with Jesus*" (Acts 4:13, emphasis mine). People will recognize when we have been with Jesus. Being with Jesus changes us and empowers us.

Given

After He called them, Jesus gave two things to His disciples: *power* and *authority*. The Greek word translated as *power* literally means "divine ability or miracle-working power." The word for *authority* means "the right or authorization to use that power." It was a delegated authority to be used as they went out in His name or as His representatives.

Why Didn't You Say So?!

Many years ago, my wife and I were in the market to buy a new car. I always hated the process of purchasing a car because in that day you had to haggle over the price. The listed price was never the actual price. It happened that the make of the car we wanted could be found at a car dealership owned by a friend of ours. He told us, "Just give the salespeople my name and they will take care of you."

We went to the dealership and told them which car we wanted. I asked for their best deal and we haggled back and forth a bit until they told me that it wasn't possible to go any lower with the sales price.

I then casually mentioned the owner's name and told them that he was a personal friend and that I was instructed by him to let them know that. The salesperson excused himself from the room (I'm sure to make a phone call confirming what I had just said). In ten minutes, he came back with a new price that was significantly lower, along with all kinds of extras and upgrades that had been thrown in for free. "Why didn't you say so?!" he asked when he came back with the new deal. "We could have saved a lot of time and given you this deal to begin with."

Things dramatically changed when I used the owner's name. He was the man in charge with the final authority. When we go out in Jesus' name, using the delegated authority He has given us, dramatic things can happen. Jesus is in charge, and there is no greater power or authority in the universe.

And it is important to remember that His power and authority are *given*, not merited or achieved. Matthew put it this way: "And when He had called His twelve disciples to Him, He *gave* them power over unclean spirits, to cast them out, and to heal all kinds of sickness and all kinds of disease. . . . 'Heal the sick, cleanse the lepers, raise the dead, cast out demons. *Freely you have received, freely give"* (Matthew 10:1, 8, emphasis mine).

Using His delegated authority, that healing power is to be ministered in the same fashion that it was received—freely.

Sent

After calling the Twelve and giving them power and authority over demons and disease, Jesus sent them out. Power and authority do no one any good if we stay at home. We must take what God has given us to the hurting people of the world. To foreign fields? Yes, but also to the local market, to the soccer field, the schools we attend, or anywhere else our lives intersect with people for whom Christ died.

Hey, My Eye!

Many years ago, when I was a relatively new Christian, I was playing a game of pick-up basketball at a local gym. It was a pretty rough game with a lot of hard fouls and pushing taking place. At one point, an off-duty marine who was playing with us got a thumb jammed in his eye. He hit the floor, writhing in pain. Eventually he stood and made his way over to a bench and sat down. I let someone else take my spot in the game and went and sat next to him. As crazy as it seemed, I felt like the Holy Spirit was telling me to pray for him.

His eye was already swollen shut, as everyone on the court could see. And frankly, I was a bit nervous about asking to pray for him. Hesitantly, I asked him if I could pray for his eye, telling him that I believed Jesus could heal him. Without hesitation, he said yes.

I put my hand on his head and prayed, while in the background I could hear some of the guys on the court snickering and laughing at me. I finished praying and sat down to watch the game. About a minute later, I heard a loud voice say, "Hey, my eye!" The marine was standing on his feet with a look of astonishment on his face. "All the pain is gone!" he said. And his eye looked perfectly normal with no swelling whatsoever. The look on the other players' faces was priceless. Everyone was stunned, and Jesus was glorified!

What Does This Have to Do with Us?

Jesus gave the Twelve power and authority and then sent them out to preach and heal. You may be thinking, *So what does that have to do with us?* The answer is *everything*.

Jesus had been preaching and healing throughout Galilee, but the job was too big, and His gracious heart was so touched with human suffering that He sent out twelve more to do the same. But still, the need was too great, and His heart was not satisfied, so in short order He sent seventy more to do the same. In fact, He sent them out in teams of two (thirty-five teams!) to preach and heal in every city and place where He was about to go (Luke 10:1–3, 8–9).

But Jesus did not stop there. His great heart was so filled with compassion for suffering, sick humanity that He called, equipped, and sent all believers with the same commission! Mark declares just prior to Christ's ascension:

> [15]And He said to them, "Go into all the world and preach the gospel to every creature. [16]He who believes and is baptized will be saved; but he who does not believe will be condemned. [17]And these signs will follow those who believe: In My name they will cast out demons; they will speak with new tongues; [18]they will take up serpents; and if they drink anything deadly, it will by no means hurt them; they will lay hands on the sick, and they will recover."

> ¹⁹So then, after the Lord had spoken to them, He was received up into heaven, and sat down at the right hand of God. ²⁰And they went out and preached everywhere, the Lord working with them and confirming the word through the accompanying signs. Amen. (Mark 16:15–20)

We need to boldly declare the same gospel, lay our hands on the sick, and expect the same results. Let us not be guilty of watering down the message or making excuses. And though we need to be ready to give an answer to any person that asks a reason for the hope that is in us, it is not our job to argue or to even to try and tackle every difficulty that may arise (1 Peter 3:15).

In Luke 9:2, it says that Jesus "sent them to preach the kingdom of God and to heal the sick." The Greek word for *preach* means "to herald." A herald is the representative of a king. The verb means "to deliver a message with authority." The business of a herald is to unapologetically proclaim the message of his king, not to field every argument or try to talk through every difficulty that someone may have with that message.

God has chosen that through the foolishness of preaching (heralding the message) those who believe the message will be delivered. The message creates faith in receptive hearts, and faith is the catalyst that releases His power to work, bringing healing, deliverance, and salvation (1 Corinthians 12:21–24; Acts 14:7–10).

Our job is to go out and boldly proclaim the truth of the gospel and to tell others about Jesus, and yes, where people are willing and receptive, to lay hands on the sick in His name. It is the Holy Spirit's job to convict people's hearts of sin and of their need for a Savior. He is the Savior and He is the Healer. We are merely humble instruments that He uses. Our part is to believe and obey. His part is to work the wonders of salvation, deliverance, and healing (Acts 16:7–11; Mark 16:20).

To Preach and Heal

It is important to notice that Jesus sent the Twelve out to preach and *then* to heal. It was the same way Jesus operated Himself. Romans 10:17 tells us, "Faith comes by hearing, and hearing by the word of God." Preaching should come first so that people can intelligently cooperate for their healing. It is through faith that miracles are received and promises are obtained (Hebrews 11:11, 33).

A Shredded Hip Socket

There was an old couple that my wife, Janet, and I became very close with. He was an evangelist who used to come and hold meetings in the church where I was an assistant pastor. After we began our own church in another town, he would come and hold meetings for us. We generally would have him preach every night for a week and pray for the sick. I still hold those meetings in my heart with the fondest of memories for all of the marvelous truths that were expounded from the Scriptures and for the amazing things that happened through prayer. The people loved him, and I especially enjoyed my personal fellowship with him as we shared meals and occasionally golfed during the afternoons. The only thing that I regret is not beating him at golf before he went to heaven!

During our times together he shared many stories with me, one of which I'd like to share with you. He was holding a two-week healing campaign in a church. They had meetings every night. On the first night, a man who was in obvious pain came forward for prayer. He walked with a severe limp due to a shredded hip socket. This was during the 1950s when hip replacement surgery was uncommon and still needed much development.

My friend, the evangelist, being led by the Holy Spirit, did not pray for the man. He sensed that the man was not ready for prayer, but rather was in need of having his faith built up through the Word. "I want you to come out to the meetings every night with your Bible and listen to the preaching, and then I will pray for your hip after two weeks," he told him. The man was not happy, but he agreed to do so. On the last night of the campaign, the man came forward for prayer. "Are you ready to be prayed for?" he was asked. "Yes, I am!" he boldly declared.

When hands were laid on him and prayer was offered, the man with the shredded hip socket suddenly screamed and then began running back and forth across the front of the church without any limp whatsoever, shouting, "I'm healed! I'm healed! God has healed me!" It was dramatic and explosive. The whole church broke out in spontaneous praise and rejoicing.

I loved hearing the story and it inspires me today, knowing that nothing is too difficult for our God. But what I hold closest to my heart is the lesson about taking in the Word of God first. This man sat every night for two weeks, in physical discomfort, listening to the Word of God preached.

His faith was enriched, strengthened, and then released to God on that final night when he was prayed for. May we never underestimate the importance of hearing good, faith-filled preaching and of personal, unhurried time in which we meditate on the Word. Proverbs 4:20–22 says it in unmistakable terms worth repeating in full:

> [20]My son, give attention to my words; incline your ear to my sayings. [21]Do not let them depart from your eyes; keep them in the midst of your heart; [22]for they are life to those who find them, and health to all their flesh.

Take Time to Replenish

"The Twelve departed and went through the towns, preaching the gospel and healing everywhere" (Luke 9:6). This didn't happen in a day or even in a week. The disciples were laboring throughout Galilee at their Lord's command. It would have been arduous and demanding work, and once they returned, they would have been tired. Luke 9:10–11 says,

> [10]And the apostles, when they had returned, told Him all that they had done. Then He took them and went aside privately into a deserted place belonging to the city called Bethsaida. [11]But when the multitudes knew it, they followed Him; and He received them and spoke to them about the kingdom of God, and healed those who had need of healing.

When they returned, they needed to rest and get replenished and Jesus knew it, so He took them aside to a deserted place to get some rest. One cannot continually pour out to others without it taking a toll. Spiritual, mental, and physical resources must be replenished or there will be an eventual crash, and that is never a pleasant thing, either for the one who has burned out or for those closest to them.

Let every believer take note, especially those who labor in the fields of preaching and pastoring—you must take time to rest. Take a weekly Sabbath (God even rested on the seventh day and He didn't need to!) and plan occasional breaks to renew and replenish both your physical and inward resources.

Vacation Interrupted

Though Jesus took His disciples to a deserted place to find some rest, their little vacation was interrupted. Somehow the multitudes found out where they were going and followed them. Was Jesus angry? No.

He compassionately spoke to them about the kingdom and continued to heal. That should give us some idea of how important our health is to the Lord. It also shows us that we should not get angry with those we are called to serve, even when they are not sensitive to our own personal needs.

A friend of mine who used to hold large tent crusades across the country once told me that he almost lost his ministry because he began to resent the people he was called to serve. He traveled a lot, which is very taxing in itself, and when he would hold his crusades in the big tent, he would preach his heart out and literally lay his hands on several thousand people for healing.

He was exhausted much of the time, but people didn't seem to consider his needs. They were so consumed with their problems and needs, they felt that they should have access to him at all times. He was tired inside and out and it took its toll on him. He became angry with the very people he was preaching to and praying for.

He shared this with me by way of admonition. God had dealt with him about his attitude (which he repented of) and his need to rest (which he began to do), and he very wisely took up a hobby, which in his words, *saved his life*. To this day, I am grateful for his advice. There is no telling where or how I might have ended up had I not heard and heeded it.

From the Mount of Glory into the Valley of Human Suffering

> [28] Now it came to pass, about eight days after these sayings, that He took Peter, John, and James and went up on the mountain to pray. [29] As He prayed, the appearance of His face was altered, and His robe became white and glistening. [30] And behold, two men talked with Him, who were Moses

> and Elijah, ³¹who appeared in glory and spoke of His decease which He was about to accomplish at Jerusalem. ³²But Peter and those with him were heavy with sleep; and when they were fully awake, they saw His glory and the two men who stood with Him. ³³Then it happened, as they were parting from Him, that Peter said to Jesus, "Master, it is good for us to be here; and let us make three tabernacles: one for You, one for Moses, and one for Elijah"—not knowing what he said. (Luke 9:28–33)

After witnessing His glory, Peter said, "Master, it is good for us to be here." That sentiment, in a way, seems to be held by many Christians. They want to stay on the mountaintop (so to speak), worshiping and basking in His glory. Spending undistracted time in the Lord's presence is essential, but as long as we are traveling through this earthly life, it is not possible to remain there indefinitely.

We are surrounded by a world that is suffering under the heel of Satan, and while it is in our power, we must do something to alleviate that suffering. Jesus took His disciples out of a divine encounter with something holy into an encounter with something very unholy.

> ³⁷Now it happened on the next day, when they had come down from the mountain, that a great multitude met Him. ³⁸Suddenly a man from the multitude cried out, saying, "Teacher, I implore You, look on my son, for he is my only child. ³⁹And behold, a spirit seizes him, and he suddenly cries out; it convulses him so that he foams at the mouth; and it departs from him with great difficulty, bruising him. ⁴⁰So I implored Your disciples to cast it out, but they could not." ⁴¹Then Jesus answered and said, "O faithless and perverse generation, how long shall I be with you and

bear with you? Bring your son here." ⁴²And as he was still coming, the demon threw him down and convulsed him. Then Jesus rebuked the unclean spirit, healed the child, and gave him back to his father. ⁴³And they were all amazed at the majesty of God. (Luke 9:37–43)

Jesus did not stay on the mountain. He came down into the valley of human suffering. Down to a distraught father whose only son was tormented by a demon. It is quite interesting that Dr. Luke uses medical terms to describe what occurred.

The word *suddenly*, used in verse 39, was used by ancient medical writers to describe sudden attacks of disease like epilepsy, and the phrase "convulses him so that he foams" is also a medical term.[1]

Yet even though Luke, the beloved physician, uses medical terms to describe the boy's condition, he emphatically states that it was the work of an unclean spirit. And the boy was not healed until the evil spirit was driven out.

It Must Not Be God's Will

Throughout the years I have, from time to time, heard people say, "I've been prayed for but nothing happened, so that means it must not be God's will to heal me."

Or something like, "Well, so and so went to this meeting or that meeting and this evangelist or pastor laid hands on them and prayed but they weren't healed, so that proves it's not God's will for them to be healed."

I have a question. What if nine of the apostles of the Lamb prayed for you? Certainly you would be healed, and if not, that would prove that it was not God's will to heal you, correct? If you agree with that, you would be wrong! While Jesus was on the mountain with Peter, James, and John, the other nine apostles tried to cast the demon out of the boy and heal him, but they failed!

And they had already been given the power and authority by Jesus to cast out demons and to heal (Luke 9:1–2). When Jesus arrived, He proved that it was God's will to set the boy free and heal him by curing him! After the boy was healed and returned to his father, everyone was amazed at the majesty, or mighty power, of God that had been displayed.

Why Did the Disciples Fail?

Why did the disciples fail? They had been empowered and authorized to set the boy free, yet they could not. To answer that question, we need to look at Matthew's account of this event. After having watched Jesus heal the boy, Matthew tells us,

> [19]Then the disciples came to Jesus privately and said, "Why could we not cast it out?" [20]So Jesus said to them, "Because of your unbelief; for assuredly, I say to you, if you have faith as a mustard seed, you will say to this mountain, 'Move from here to there,' and it will move; and nothing will be impossible for you. [21]However, this kind does not go out except by prayer and fasting." (Matthew 17:19–21)

Jesus very clearly told them that the reason for their failure was their lack of faith and then added that this type of evil spirit cannot be cast out without spiritual preparation. In fact, I think we can look at the text this way without doing any harm to the spirit of what Jesus is saying: "This kind of *unbelief* only goes out by prayer and fasting." When we fast and pray, the body becomes quiet and we can more readily hear the voice of God, which is where faith comes from (Romans 10:17).

Jesus had been on the mountain praying before He came upon the scene with the demonized boy, but Peter, James, and John had been sleeping (Luke 9:29–32). Jesus was prepared. Had the nine disciples at the bottom of the mountain been sleeping as well? One thing is for sure—they had not been fasting and praying.

Demon at a Bible Study

Years ago, I held a weekly Bible study in the home of some friends. We regularly saw God do amazing things as we prayed for the sick. A new group of people who had begun attending told me of a childhood friend they had had whom they were certain was demonized. They said he was given to violent, irrational outbursts and would say crazy nonsensical things. He continually disrupted any gathering he was at and was especially antagonistic toward anything that had to do with Jesus. They then asked if they could bring him to the next week's Bible study. "Of course," I said. "Bring him."

Though all believers have been given authority over Satan and demons in Jesus' name (Mark 16:17; Ephesians 1:17–23), I had the distinct impression to prepare my heart. So, over the next couple of days I did some fasting and spent some extra time in prayer and in the Word.

When Bible study night rolled around, the people's "guest" did not disappoint. Within minutes of starting, he began to loudly challenge me and then he rose and aggressively came toward me. I was prepared. I spoke the name of Jesus and commanded the demon to leave him. His transformation was immediate and recognizable by all. His countenance and demeanor were instantly altered. The rage was replaced by peace and what I can only describe as bewilderment. He was changed in an instant and spent the rest of the evening hungrily listening to God's Word.

Three Persons Involved in Your Healing

Even though the Scriptures reveal many different ways that God has healed people, most generally, there are three distinct persons involved when someone receives divine healing: *God, you, and the person who prays for you* or lays hands on you.

God has made His will clear in the matter of healing. We could say that He has written His will in blood across the back of Jesus with a Roman whip. By His stripes we are healed (Isaiah 53:5; 1 Peter 2:24). The truth is God has *already* done something about our healing.

When seeking healing, *you* must be ready and be in faith. That is done by hearing and agreeing with the gospel message on healing. It is important to be ready and receptive rather than just curious or wishful. Many people touched Jesus as He was on His way to the house of Jairus, but only the touch of faith drew healing power out of Him (Luke 8:43–46).

Did You Turn the Key On?

One day some friends and I tried to help a lady push start her car when her battery had died. She had a manual transmission, so we thought it would only take a minute to get her going. There shouldn't have been a problem, yet even though we got the car briskly rolling numerous times, when she popped the clutch and put it in gear, it wouldn't start.

We were all kind of baffled and I finally said, "Let me try." She agreed, and when I climbed into the driver's seat, I noticed that the key was turned off. "Did you turn the key on?" I asked. "Oh," she responded. "Does it need to be on?" My friends and I looked at one another and laughed, as we all said, "Yes, it does!"

I think that many people who come up in a prayer line or make some sort of request for healing prayer are sort of like that woman with the car. They are expecting someone else's prayer alone to push them through to healing. They don't realize that their faith, like that car key, must be turned on. When it comes to receiving healing, the individual in need should be believing and expecting based on what they personally know the Scriptures to say.

Finally, the person who prays for you or lays hands on you must be in faith and must be right with God. This whole story (recorded in Luke 9 and Matthew 17) teaches us that the boy was not healed because the disciples were not prepared. Jesus, however, was prepared, and He cast the demon out of the boy, curing him.

CHAPTER

10

Bound by Satan, Freed by Christ

And He was casting out a demon, and it was mute. So it was, when the demon had gone out, that the mute spoke; and the multitudes marveled. (Luke 11:14)

An evil spirit was affecting this person's vocal faculties, rendering them speechless. Matthew gives us a fuller picture as he relates that the person was both blind and mute. Once the demon was expelled by Jesus, the person was able to both see and speak. This act of casting out the demon and curing the person was apparently done publicly, as the multitudes marveled at it.

Again, Matthew adds a bit more color and texture to the story as he also states that upon seeing this healing occur, the multitudes began to ask, "Could this be the Son of David?" which was a very common term for the Messiah (Matthew 12:22–23).

> But some of them said, "He casts out demons by Beelzebub, the ruler of the demons." (Luke 11:15)

After hearing the multitudes begin to ask such questions, the Pharisees (Matthew 11:24) accused Jesus of being in league with Beelzebub (a term used by the Jews for the devil). Imagine! They did not rejoice because a blind and mute man could now see and speak. They were not filled with wonder at the amazing healing that had just occurred before their eyes.

They had become willfully blind in their jealousy and poisoned by their bitterness to the point that they were willing to attribute the clear work of the Holy Spirit to Satan.

In His next few statements, Jesus tells them in no uncertain terms that a divided house will fall, even if that house is Satan's. The devil is not working against himself. The calamity was from Satan, but the cure was from the Holy Spirit. Satan had bound the man with blindness and muteness, but Jesus had set him free. Jesus came to give us abundant life, but the thief *only* comes to kill, steal, and to destroy (John 10:10).

Flicked Away like a Piece of Lint

In His declarations to His accusers, Jesus states, "But if I cast out demons with the finger of God, surely the kingdom of God has come upon you" (Luke 11:20).

The finger of God is synonymous with the Holy Spirit (Matthew 12:28), yet by rendering it this way, Luke teaches us a great lesson. When Jesus cast the demon out of this person, restoring their sight and speech, it was no titanic struggle among equals. It was done by the finger of God. As easily as one would flick away a piece of lint, Jesus cast the demon out. Satan stands no chance against the power of God.

²¹"When a strong man, fully armed, guards his own palace, his goods are in peace. ²²But when a stronger than he comes upon him and overcomes him, he takes from him all his armor in which he trusted, and divides his spoils." (Luke 11:21–22)

Jesus is the stronger One who has overcome the devil and divided his spoils. We, as members of the body of Christ, are made partakers of His victory. When we submit ourselves to God and resist the devil, he will flee from us. The greater One resides in us, and we have been authorized to use His name (James 4:7; 1 John 4:4; Mark 16:17; 1 John 2:13).

How Can You Tell?

Luke makes it clear that this person's muteness and blindness were being caused by a demon. The person could not have been cured until that demonic entity had been cast out. It is something that we have seen several times in his Gospel narrative already, yet not all (or even most) illnesses are caused and enforced by the presence of an evil spirit.

Where that is the case, the demon must be dealt with before healing can occur, but how can you tell? How can you be certain that a demon is present? If you are just guessing, it would be like taking a shot in the dark, and you could not truly operate in faith by just guessing.

The only way to know for sure is through the aid of the Holy Spirit. The gifts of the discerning of spirits and the word of knowledge can both be used to reveal the presence of an evil spirit, and it is through the aid of the Holy Spirit that those gifts operate (1 Corinthians 12:7–11).

If the Holy Spirit (through one of these gifts) does not reveal that an evil spirit is present, either causing or enforcing an illness, then we must treat it as a natural illness that can be healed through the laying on of hands or through the prayer of faith (Mark 16:18; James 5:14–15).

A Black Monkey on His Lung

Many years ago, I was holding a series of healing meetings in a small rural town in California. Every night, I preached on healing and prayed for the sick. One evening, something very unusual happened.

Everyone had stood to their feet as I was praying for someone in the front of the auditorium. While I was laying my hands on the person who had come forward for prayer, I happened to glance at a family standing together a few rows back. When I looked at them, their teenage son suddenly seemed to become partially transparent. It was a manifestation of the discerning of spirits.

I had not expected it to happen, it just did. As I looked at him, I could see both of his lungs, and clinging to one of them was something that looked to me like a little black monkey. I turned to the family and asked, "Does your son have something wrong with one of his lungs?" "Yes," his father said, looking astonished. "He has tuberculosis in one of his lungs."

Without hesitation, I spoke in the name of Jesus to the evil spirit to release his lung, and as I watched, it fell to the floor. "Leave this place in Jesus' name!" I commanded it. It scampered down the center aisle and disappeared.

No one else saw what I saw, and nothing like that has ever happened to me again, but I knew the boy was healed. The next night, that family was back at the meeting and they were beaming. They had gone to the doctor that day and insisted that new X-rays be taken of his lungs.

They were completely clear with no trace of tuberculosis! Glory be to God! That young man went on to become a pastor. I ran into him at a ministers meeting thirty years later and he told me that he had recently had a chest X-ray due to a car accident he had been in. "There is still no sign of that tuberculosis," he said. "God healed me that night and I have stayed healed all these years!"

A Spirit of Infirmity

Our beloved physician evangelist Luke now brings us to another striking incident where Jesus heals someone with a physical malady that had been caused by an evil spirit.

> [10]Now He was teaching in one of the synagogues on the Sabbath. [11]And behold, there was a woman who had a spirit of infirmity eighteen years, and was bent over and could in no way raise herself up. [12]But when Jesus saw her, He called her to Him and said to her, "Woman, you are loosed from your infirmity." [13]And He laid His hands on her, and immediately she was made straight, and glorified God. (Luke 13:10–13)

Again, it is worth noting that Jesus was in the synagogue *teaching*. That was His method everywhere—teaching before healing. May we never underestimate the absolute importance of sitting under good teaching. His Word produces faith in receptive hearts.

As the story unfolds, Luke uses medical terms to describe the terrible condition of a woman in the synagogue. He tells us that she was *bent over* and that she could in no way *raise herself up*.

Both of these are medical terms meaning that she was literally bent over double and could not so much as raise her head to look up because of her condition. Yet even though Luke describes her physical condition medically, he emphatically states that it was the work of an evil spirit. The true cause of her malady could not be found under a microscope or by examining some lab specimen.

She had a *spirit of infirmity*, or we could literally say a *spirit of sickness*. There are certain kinds of spirits that do nothing but make people sick. Just like there are unclean spirits and lying spirits, there are sickness spirits. This one slowly made this poor woman's back curve until she was completely bent over. That spirit had afflicted her for eighteen years!

It Jumped on My Hands

I remember years ago listening to a minister that I greatly respected (who later became a dear friend) share a story I shall never forget. He was ministering in a church and near the end of the service he had people come forward who desired prayer for healing.

A couple came forward and the wife requested prayer for her hands. They were terribly twisted and deformed. She said that her hands used to be perfectly fine until one day she felt something *jump* on them (her words). After that, her hands began to have a burning sensation and slowly, over the next several years, they began to twist and deform. They tried hand braces and other things, but nothing worked.

"When my hands got like they are now, I felt that thing jump off of my hands." "Yes," said her husband as he withdrew his hands from his pockets. "And then it jumped on my hands." His hands were twisted and gnarled in the same way that his wife's were. That was unquestionably the work of a spirit of infirmity.

Woman, You Are Loosed

When Jesus saw the woman, he called her and said, "Woman, you are loosed from your infirmity" (v. 12). The Greek word translated *loosed* literally means to "dismiss" or to "send away."

That was when Jesus dealt with the spirit that was afflicting her, but even though it departed, its effects still remained (eighteen years' worth!).

So now, in order to bring a miraculous physical restoration, Jesus laid His hands on her. When He did, she was immediately made straight and glorified God. It is important to remember that it was her healing that brought glory to God, not eighteen years of demonically enforced sickness. What happens next is hard to comprehend.

> But the ruler of the synagogue answered with indignation, because Jesus had healed on the Sabbath; and he said to the crowd, "There are six days on which men ought to work; therefore come and be healed on them, and not on the Sabbath day." (Luke 13:14)

Imagine the scene. Everyone in the synagogue knew this woman. She had suffered for eighteen years, bent over double, having to scoot along like some giant spider. Then, at a word and a touch from Jesus, she is suddenly, gloriously, made whole. Standing perfectly straight, she is singing the praises of God, and the ruler of the synagogue is mad!

This ruler more than likely knew her through all of the years of her misery. He had watched as some evil entity slowly forced her body to bend unnaturally until it was completely misshapen. Every Sabbath she was present in the assembly, unable to raise herself up or look anyone in the eye.

Now she is healed and giving God the credit, and all the ruler can do is cry foul! He even tried to turn the crowd against Jesus, saying that he had healed on the wrong day! Any other day is fine to come and be healed, but not on the Sabbath!

In essence, he was saying that Jesus reaching out His hand was work, and the woman standing up straight was work, and you're not supposed to work on the Sabbath day! The utter ridiculousness of it, as well as his pompous indignation, is hard to fathom. It also seems like he was trying to discourage anyone else from coming forward to receive healing, which is wicked, in my opinion.

Hypocrite!

> [15]The Lord then answered him and said, "Hypocrite! Does not each one of you on the Sabbath loose his ox or donkey from the stall, and lead it away to water it? [16]So ought not this woman, being a daughter of Abraham, whom Satan has bound—think of it—for eighteen years, be loosed from this bond on the Sabbath?" [17]And when He said these things, all His adversaries were put to shame; and all the multitude rejoiced for all the glorious things that were done by Him. (Luke 13:15–17)

Paraphrased, Jesus told him, "You say my lifting my hand to heal her is wrong on the Sabbath, and yet you don't hesitate to lift your hand to help an ox or a donkey on the Sabbath!" And in answering him, Jesus used the ruler's own language to bring out the truth of the situation. Jesus said that the ruler (as well as several other adversaries present) would *loose* his ox or donkey from the stall. He basically said that the ruler would rather see a donkey loosed and helped than a woman in the congregation loosed and helped!

The ruler also said that there are six days on which men *ought* to work. Jesus used the man's own word as He basically said, "You say, *ought*? I'll tell you what *ought* to be done. This woman *ought* to be healed since she is a daughter of Abraham!" When Jesus had finished with them, all of His adversaries were ashamed and the multitude was rejoicing.

Thoughts to Ponder

"So ought not this woman, being a daughter of Abraham, whom Satan has bound—think of it—for eighteen years, be loosed from this bond on the Sabbath?" (Luke 13:16)

As Jesus answered the hypocritical ruler, He said to *think*. Following are some thoughts about this story worth pondering.

1. Jesus said that the woman had been bound by Satan. Sickness is from the devil. Here, in this particular instance, it is in a direct sense, but all sickness, at least indirectly, finds its source in Satan. Acts 10:38 declares, "How God anointed Jesus of Nazareth with the Holy Spirit and with power, who went about doing good and **healing all who were oppressed by the devil**, for God was with Him" (emphasis mine). The People's New Testament commentary on this story from Luke 13 puts it well when it says, "All disease is the offspring of sin, but from Satan came sin."[1]

2. The woman afflicted with this terrible condition was in the synagogue, a house of worship. She was there to hear the Word of God and to worship. Apparently, she was not bitter at God or blaming Him for her condition, which we can see would have been placing the blame where it did not belong. Satan had bound her, not God. As long as we blame or accuse God, we will not likely find deliverance from His hand.

3. Jesus said she ought to be healed. Why? Because she was a daughter of Abraham. She had a covenant with God, which included healing. This directly relates to all who have given their lives to Christ, for Galatians 3:29 declares, "***And if you are Christ's, then you are Abraham's seed, and heirs according to the promise.***"

In his writings, the apostle Paul makes it clear that from heaven's standpoint, the highest quality that makes us children of Abraham is our faith. In Romans 4, he talks about walking in the footsteps of Abraham's faith, who, when there was no natural reason for hope continued to believe. Abraham had to hang on to God's promise for twenty-five years before eventually experiencing its fulfillment.

This woman, for part of or perhaps all eighteen years, had no doubt been clinging to God's promises. She would have heard them repeatedly read in the synagogue:

> The Lord opens the eyes of the blind; the Lord raises those who are bowed down; the Lord loves the righteous. (Psalm 146:8)
>
> He sent His word and healed them, and delivered them from their destructions. (Psalm 107:20)
>
> [1]Bless the Lord, O my soul; and all that is within me, bless His holy name! [2]Bless the Lord, O my soul, and forget not all His benefits: [3]who forgives all your iniquities, who heals all your diseases. (Psalm 103:1–3)
>
> "I am the Lord who heals you." (Exodus 15:26)
>
> "So you shall serve the Lord your God, and He will bless your bread and your water. And I will take sickness away from the midst of you." (Exodus 23:25)

This is so significant. If you have been standing in faith for a long time, clinging to a promise, don't give up! As surely as Jesus saw her, He sees you, and He is still the same compassionate Healer today as He was that day in the synagogue. Put your trust in Him alone.

Go Tell That Fox

> ³¹On that very day some Pharisees came, saying to Him, "Get out and depart from here, for Herod wants to kill You." ³²And He said to them, "Go, tell that fox, 'Behold, I cast out demons and perform cures today and tomorrow, and the third day I shall be perfected.'" (Luke 13:31–32)

The Pharisees were not suddenly concerned for Jesus' safety. Though the threat from Herod was no doubt real, their motive for informing Jesus of it at this time was as impure as they were. It was a ploy to get rid of Him. Jesus had shamed them, and the people were rejoicing at all the glorious things that were done by Him.

Jesus gave them a message for Herod. First, He referred to Herod as a fox. More specifically, Jesus called him a female fox.² It was a term of contempt. Apparently, Herod was so reprobate that he deserved such a title.

He had murdered John, and though he earnestly wanted to see Jesus, the Lord utterly avoided him. Even when Pilate later sent Jesus to Herod, Jesus refused to speak to him. It is a sad commentary on the level of depravity that a person's soul can reach when the Lord Himself refuses to speak to you directly and the only indirect message He sends is one of distaste and contempt.

Included in that message for Herod was a clear declaration of what Jesus would continue to do as He headed for Jerusalem, where He would be *perfected* (v. 32). That is a term He used to refer to His death on the cross as our substitute. In fact, it is a form of the word Jesus used on the cross when He said, "It is finished" (John 19:30).

As Jesus progressed toward the completion of our redemption, He would continue to cast out demons and perform cures. Healing was not some side issue that Jesus occasionally addressed. He actively healed the sick right up until He was unjustly arrested and crucified.

As we continue journeying with Jesus to His cross, Luke tells us in detail about several more of those cures that Jesus performed along the way.

CHAPTER

11

Healing on the Sabbath . . . Again

¹Now it happened, as He went into the house of one of the rulers of the Pharisees to eat bread on the Sabbath, that they watched Him closely. ²And behold, there was a certain man before Him who had dropsy. ³And Jesus, answering, spoke to the lawyers and Pharisees, saying, "Is it lawful to heal on the Sabbath?" ⁴But they kept silent. And He took him and healed him, and let him go. ⁵Then He answered them, saying, "Which of you, having a donkey or an ox that has fallen into a pit, will not immediately pull him out on the Sabbath day?" ⁶And they could not answer Him regarding these things. (Luke 14:1–6)

According to verse 12 of this chapter, Jesus had been invited to the house of the ruler of the Pharisees. This ruler, along with others, had asked Him to join them to eat bread on that Sabbath, not out of a spirit of hospitality, but rather to set a trap.

There was a man there (either invited or brought in) who had dropsy. Again, Luke uses a medical term to describe the man's condition. It is derived from the Greek word for water. It referred to a very painful condition where fluid (or water) surrounded inflamed joints, as well as generally making a person's facial features appear puffy and distorted.

The lawyers and Pharisees watched Jesus closely with ill intent (which is the meaning in the original language), hoping that He would heal on the Sabbath day so that they could accuse Him. The truth was they had no real concern about doctrinal integrity or the sanctity of the Sabbath.

Their defense of the faith and stand for correct doctrine was just a smokescreen for their real motivation. They wanted to discredit Jesus or get Him out of the way because they were envious. In a short time, when they would hand Him over to Pilate, even he would recognize that they had done so out of envy (Matthew 27:18).

The events we are reading about now all take place near the very end of Jesus' ministry. Many of the Jewish religious leaders' hearts had been boiling over with hatred for Him for some time now, even to the point where a group of them here were willing to use the guise of hospitality to snare Him.

So, their snare is set. They have brought in the man suffering from a very recognizable and painful disease, not because they care for him, but because they needed bait for their trap. That was all he was to them.

They would rather pull their donkey out of a pit than see this man pulled out of a pit of pain and sickness. In fact, Jesus made it clear that their response to the donkey or ox would be *immediate* (even on the Sabbath), but with this man, there would be nothing but refusal if it were in their power to help him.

They Would Not, Then They Could Not

In verse 3, it says that Jesus *answered* the lawyers and Pharisees, yet they never spoke a word. He answered their action of putting the diseased man before Him as bait for their trap, and He answered their attitudes and uncaring hearts. In fact, Jesus answered them with the same question that they had previously put to Him, "**Is it lawful to heal on the Sabbath**?" (Matthew 12:10).

Their response to His question was to keep silent. They refused to answer. But in reality, their refusal to answer was an answer. So after healing the man, He responded to them again (vv. 4–5), but this time *they could not answer* (v. 6).

First they *would not* answer, then they *could not* answer. There is a principle here worth noting. It is what happened to Pharaoh when the exodus took place. First, he would not soften his heart and then he could not soften his heart. In this story of the man healed of dropsy, Jesus is very mercifully dealing with the hearts of those trying to entrap Him. He is giving them space to yield to the truth, but they refuse. *They should have when they could have, but because they wouldn't, eventually they couldn't.*

False Teaching! False Prophet!

Years ago, a traveling evangelist came to the small town in Oregon where I was living. I was personally at every single meeting the evangelist held, and they were wonderful. The Scriptures were being expounded upon, and people were being saved and healed regularly.

There was actually quite a buzz about the meetings in town, and the numbers of those attending began to swell. Most everyone was excited . . . except one man in particular. He was an ordained Christian minister who had spent many years in training. He held Bible studies, but almost no one attended. He had an air of arrogant authority, claiming to be the most knowledgeable Bible scholar in town. Most people just avoided him.

He began to actively denounce the evangelist and his teaching, calling him a false prophet, even though he had never attended a single meeting personally. He did all he could to sow distrust in the hearts of the people about the evangelist, yet the crowds continued to grow.

Finally, one evening he came out to a meeting personally, but it was not to worship or to receive teaching. It was solely for the purpose of catching the evangelist in his words so he could have something *firsthand* to accuse him of. I was present at the meeting.

It was the largest one to date and the atmosphere was filled with faith. I guess it was more than the Bible scholar could take because just as the evangelist began his teaching, this man stood to his feet and began to loudly shout, "*False teaching! False Prophet!*" It was obvious that the man's denunciation was being fueled by envy. As the man continued to shout and disrupt the meeting, the evangelist just calmly asked everyone to stand and lift our hands and begin to praise the Lord, which we did. The man promptly ran out of the building.

I was aware of several people who knew the man who tried to talk to him, but he wouldn't listen. I tried to talk to him, but he wouldn't listen. Over the next several months, he grew angrier and more bitter at everyone, and he was eventually even asked to leave the ministry that had originally invited him to town to help them.

I'm sure there were moments where the Lord graciously dealt with him about the posture of his heart, but apparently, he did not heed them. He reminded me of the Pharisees and lawyers in Luke 14 whose hearts had become so calloused that they went from refusing to answer to being unable to answer.

Think of the Poor Man

Think of the poor man with the dropsy. He had to have known why he had been brought there. He must have felt like a rabbit with a tethered leg, set out as bait to catch the hawk.

If we could have looked into his pleading eyes, they would have told it all: *"I'm sorry, Jesus. I know what they're doing, but I need You! I'm suffering so! I hate being set out as bait by those jealous men. I know they despise me and care nothing for me . . . but I believe You can help me. Please, Jesus!"*

And Jesus, wonderful, compassionate Jesus, healed him and let him go. The rabbit was released from its captors! And the hard hearts that would invite Jesus to share a meal in order to snare Him were reproved.

A Type of Christ

Jesus healed this man on the Sabbath, but that was not unusual. Jesus healed many people on the Sabbath. In fact, it seems that He purposely did so.

In Luke 4, Jesus cast out a demon, healed Peter's mother-in-law, and healed a vast multitude—all on the Sabbath. He healed a man with a withered hand (Luke 6), He healed the woman who was bent over (Luke 13), He healed a man who had been sick for thirty-eight years (John 5), and He healed a man born blind (John 9)—all on the Sabbath.

The Sabbath was to be a day of rest, a day devoted to God where no work was to be done. As an example to us, after having completed the work of creation, even God rested on the Sabbath (Genesis 2:2).

But as well as being designed for man's benefit (Mark 2:27), the Sabbath was a type of Christ. It found its fulfillment in Him (Colossians 2:16–17). God finished our redemption through Jesus' suffering and death. Nothing more remains to be done but to believe and to enter into rest . . . even when it comes to healing.

The work has been done! Healing is a part of the inheritance and rest that God has provided for His people through Christ, which Jesus demonstrated time and time again by healing on the Sabbath.

Speaking about the inheritance of the Promised Land, which God had promised (hence the designation *Promised* Land) to bring His people into, the Scriptures plainly tell us that some did not experience it because of unbelief.

> And to whom did He swear that they would not enter His rest, but to those who did not obey? So we see that they could not enter in because of unbelief. (Hebrews 3:18–19)

The next few verses in Hebrews are very illuminating. They tell us,

> Therefore, since a promise remains of entering His rest, let us fear lest any of you seem to have come short of it. For indeed the gospel was preached to us as well as to them; but the word which they heard did not profit them, not being mixed with faith in those who heard it. For we who have believed do enter that rest, as He has said: "So I swore in My wrath, 'They shall not enter My rest,'" although the works were finished from the foundation of the world. (Hebrews 4:1–3)

Then in verse 11 we are told, "Let us therefore be diligent to enter that rest, lest anyone fall according to the same example of disobedience." I especially like the King James Version of that verse. It reads, "Let us labour therefore to enter into that rest."

That labor that brings us into our inheritance and everything that rest implies is *the labor of faith*. The Scripture clearly reveals that it is through faith that we enter into that rest. I encourage you to prayerfully read all of Hebrews 4.

You will find that it tells us that we enter into our rest, that is, we possess all that Christ died and suffered to provide by taking God at His Word. As we believe it and act upon it, we enter into that rest.

There are some notes from the Ryrie Study Bible on this that are quite good and I have included them here. "Rest in the Christian life comes through complete reliance on God's promises and full surrender to His will. Joshua (Moses' successor) could not lead all the people into the rest of dwelling in their promised land because of their unbelief. Likewise, the believer today cannot enjoy a fully satisfying life unless he believes all the promises of God."[1]

Brother Mitchell

When we believe, we enter that rest. There is no struggling, no earning, just resting in what God's Word declares that Christ has already accomplished. The best example I can think of to illustrate this happened with a member of our congregation. I never knew his first name, but everyone just called him Brother Mitchell.

One Sunday morning after service, Brother Mitchell came up to me requesting prayer. "Sure," I responded. "What are we praying about?" I asked. "I just came from the doctor and I have been diagnosed with cancer," he said.

We prayed together and then he lifted his hands and praised God for a minute or so, thanking Him for hearing us and sending the answer. I'd like to tell you that I followed up with Brother Mitchell after we prayed, but honestly, I got busy with everything going on at church and didn't think about him for several weeks . . . that is until I saw him in service again.

Once the service ended, I went up to him (feeling bad because I hadn't called him or looked into his situation since we prayed) and asked, "How are you doing, Brother Mitchell? Any word on the cancer situation?"

"Well," he said, "after we prayed I just sort of forgot about it, that is, until I had another doctor's appointment about a week later. When they checked me, they couldn't find the cancer anywhere. It was gone. The Lord healed me." I was stunned.

Not because he had been healed, but because he *just sort of forgot* about his cancer diagnosis! To this day it encourages me to rest in the Lord once I have taken ahold of one of His promises by faith.

The next story that Luke relates of Jesus healing the sick illustrates in a beautiful way what it really means to have faith in His Word. It actually is the story of ten men that had to *labor* to enter that rest.

The Ten Lepers

> [11]Now it happened as He went to Jerusalem that He passed through the midst of Samaria and Galilee. [12]Then as He entered a certain village, there met Him ten men who were lepers, who stood afar off. [13]And they lifted up their voices and said, "Jesus, Master, have mercy on us!"
>
> [14]So when He saw them, He said to them, "Go, show yourselves to the priests." And so it was that as they went, they were cleansed.
>
> [15]And one of them, when he saw that he was healed, returned, and with a loud voice glorified God, [16]and fell down on his face at His feet, giving Him thanks. And he was a Samaritan.

¹⁷So Jesus answered and said, "Were there not ten cleansed? But where are the nine? ¹⁸Were there not any found who returned to give glory to God except this foreigner?" ¹⁹And He said to him, "Arise, go your way. Your faith has made you well." (Luke 17:11–19)

Going Against the Grain

It is worth noting that as Jesus was slowly making His way to Jerusalem, He passed through the midst of (or along the border between) Samaria and Galilee. Earlier, when Jesus had sent messengers before Him into a Samaritan village to prepare for Him, that village did not receive, welcome, or accept Him (Luke 9:52–53).

We must be careful whose influence we come under. It could cause us to lose out with God or fail to receive the blessings He is freely offering. These ten men dared to go against the grain, refusing to adopt the prevailing attitude of some of their fellow countrymen. If they had not, their story would not be recorded for us to learn from.

Did you notice that the lepers *met Him*? They must have been seeking Him out. No doubt they heard the wonderful story of Jesus previously healing the man who was full of leprosy (Luke 5:12–14), and I'm sure it would have thrilled their souls and been the beginning spark for their faith.

Yet, coming to Jesus would have been no easy task for them. They were forbidden to mingle with the general public, so getting fresh news about Jesus' whereabouts or even traveling to where they thought He might turn up would have been extremely difficult, but they still managed to find Him!

When they had discovered where He was, they came out *to meet* Him, but they did not actually come close to Him. Even as the law of Moses commanded, they stood afar off (Leviticus 13:45–46), and from a distance they called out for mercy. In the end, their labor was rewarded.

Have Mercy on Us

When these ten men lifted their voices to Jesus, they didn't cry out for justice or equality and they did not accuse God of being unfair. They didn't say, "What did we ever do to deserve this? Do you know how much we have suffered? We have lost family and friends. We cannot work, we are in constant pain. We are isolated and lonely. How could a just God allow this to happen?"

No, they cried out for *mercy*! It has been said that only the guilty need mercy. And thank God, the Lord is full of mercy, and healing, as well as forgiveness, is a manifestation of God's mercy. As New Testament believers, we are told to "come boldly to the throne of grace that you may obtain mercy and find grace to help in time of need" (Psalm 86:15; 145:8; Mark 10:46–52; Hebrews 4:16).

As well as humbling themselves and asking for mercy, they also addressed Jesus as *Master*. If you are expecting help from the Lord, you must first settle the issue of who is the master of your life. Submit your heart completely to Him and then come humbly yet boldly to His throne of grace. He has mercy and favor in abundance to bestow on all those who come in this fashion.

You Can't Put God in a Box

When Jesus healed the man of leprosy in Luke 5, He touched him. The man's leprosy instantly left, and then Jesus told him to go and show himself to the priest (it was the priest's job to examine a leper who had been healed and officially pronounce them clean). In this case, the men were told to go and show themselves to the priests *before* their leprosy had disappeared.

Why did the Lord choose a different method here? We are not told, but when it comes to how the Lord works our healing, you can't put God in a box. He works all things after the counsel of His own will. Our part is to believe His word and obey Him. His part is to work the cure in whatever way and through whatever means He sees fit.

They Acted Upon His Word Alone

When Jesus told the ten lepers to go to the priests, they had no physical evidence whatsoever that they were healed. They were cured *as they went*. In essence, Jesus was saying, "You are healed now and you must act in faith if it is going to be manifested."

They might have argued, "Wait, Jesus. We heard about the other guy You healed of leprosy. You're supposed to touch us like You did him! This is the wrong way! You healed the other guy and then You sent Him to the priest. Everyone could see that his leprosy had vanished. He had the evidence before he went." But the truth was they had all the evidence they needed—the word of Jesus! Like these lepers, we need to accept His word on the subject of our healing, or any other thing, and go on our way believing.

It Happened Four Nights Ago

An old friend of mine used to work the cameras for a prominent US evangelist during the late 1950s. The meetings were held under a tent seating thousands and the services were generally full. My friend told me of a man who came forward for prayer one night. He had a large cancerous growth on his face that marred his features severely. He was prayed for and then went and sat back down.

The next night they had a time for testimonies, where people who had been healed came up to the microphone and shared their stories. This man got in the testimony line with the growth still clinging savagely to his face. When it was his turn, he got up and testified that he had been healed the night before when the evangelist laid hands on him and prayed for him.

No one clapped. It was an awkward moment, because everyone could clearly see that he was *not* healed. The growth was still on his face.

He did the same thing the next night with the same response from the people. The next night, he did the same thing. The following night he came up as well, but this time, the growth was missing! He had it with him in a jar! He said as he was shaving around the growth that evening to get ready to come to the service that it just fell off of his face into the sink and in its place was new, perfect looking skin.

As he shared that night the place went wild! Everyone was shouting and many asked, "When did it happen?" His response was, "It happened four nights ago when the evangelist laid hands on me."

The Title Deed

> Now faith is the assurance (the confirmation, the title deed) of the things [we] hope for, being the proof of things [we] do not see and the conviction of their reality [faith perceiving as real fact what is not revealed to the senses]. (Hebrews 11:1 AMPC)

Faith deals with unseen realities. If you can see it, touch it, or handle it, you don't need faith for it. Faith takes the promise of God, embraces it, and acts like it is a reality. Faith is the *title deed* to the things we are trusting God for. Until the healing that I have prayed for arrives in physical form, I hold firmly to the title deed of faith. His promise is my assurance. His promise (or declaration) is sufficient evidence. His Word is the basis for my faith.

Once, a couple deeded a small property to our church. All of the proper paperwork was done and the ownership was transferred to us. We had not seen the property or ever walked on it. We didn't even have a picture of it, but it was ours.

How could we be sure? We had the title deed! We eventually sold it and put the money into missions, all without ever seeing the property! Someone might have called us crazy or extreme, but we declared that the property was ours and acted like it was so, and the only evidence we had was words written on some papers by fallible men.

May we have at least that much faith in the written words of our infallible God. The ten lepers acted upon the word of Jesus, and as they did, their healing moved from the unseen (faith) realm to the realm of sight and touch where everyone could see what had happened.

One Returned

When the lepers began making their way to the priests, their bodies were still leprous. As they went, they were cleansed. On the way, when one of them suddenly realized that his leprosy had vanished, he decided to return to Jesus. He loudly glorified God, fell at Jesus' feet, and thanked Him.

Jesus' response was revealing. He knew all ten had been healed, and asked, "Where are the other nine?" Those who lift their voice in prayer should also lift up their voice in praise. Are we among the nine? Or are we in the category of the one that returned to offer thanks? The ratio may still be true today. May we strive to offer thanks for all the good that God has done for us.

I have heard it asked: "If all you had today is what you thanked God for yesterday, how much would you have?" It is a question worth pondering.

CHAPTER

12

Mercy, Mercy, and More Mercy

In the last chapter, we saw how the ten lepers cried out for mercy and received it in the form of healing. God's mercy is a fountain that never runs dry. Now, as we come to chapter 18, again we find Jesus extending the mercy of healing to someone in need.

> ³⁵Then it happened, as He was coming near Jericho, that a certain blind man sat by the road begging. ³⁶And hearing a multitude passing by, he asked what it meant. ³⁷So they told him that Jesus of Nazareth was passing by. ³⁸And he cried out, saying, "Jesus, Son of David, have mercy on me!" ³⁹Then those who went before warned him that he should be quiet; but he cried out all the more, "Son of David, have mercy on me!" ⁴⁰So Jesus stood still and commanded him to be brought to Him. And when he had come near, He asked him, ⁴¹saying, "What do you want Me to do for you?" He said, "Lord, that I may receive my sight." ⁴²Then Jesus said to him, "Receive your sight; your faith has made you well." ⁴³And immediately he received his sight, and followed Him, glorifying God. And all the people, when they saw it, gave praise to God. (Luke 18:35–43)

Once again, just like with the healed leper who returned to give thanks, Jesus said to the now-healed blind man, "*Your faith has made you well.*" But what did he have faith in? You say, "Faith in Jesus," and you are right, but more specifically, he had faith in the Lord's mercy and faith in His promises.

Not a Sudden Thing

This blind man's faith was not a sudden thing. It had grown over a period of time. Jesus was a very common name, but when he heard that it was *Jesus of Nazareth* passing by, that was different. It was Jesus the miracle worker. This blind man had obviously heard how He had healed multitudes . . . including many who had been blind. He had thought deeply about it. Alone in his darkness, he had pondered the stories about this Jesus of Nazareth for months, maybe even for years. He came to the conclusion that this Jesus was the Messiah, and he gave Him a full messianic title, "*Son of David.*"

Like every Jew, he knew the promises about the coming Messiah, such as Isaiah 35:4–5, which says, "Say to those who are fearful-hearted, 'Be strong, do not fear! Behold, your God will come with vengeance, with the recompense of God; He will come and save you.' Then the eyes of the blind shall be opened, and the ears of the deaf shall be unstopped."

And Isaiah 42:6–7, which declares of the Messiah, "I, the Lord, have called You in righteousness, and will hold Your hand; I will keep You and give You as a covenant to the people, as a light to the Gentiles, to open blind eyes, to bring out prisoners from the prison, those who sit in darkness from the prison house."

Perhaps he was even aware of Jesus' own claim when He quoted in the synagogue from Isaiah 61 about Himself saying,

> ¹⁸"The Spirit of the Lord is upon Me, because He has anointed Me to preach the gospel to the poor; He has sent Me to heal the brokenhearted, to proclaim liberty to the captives and recovery of sight to the blind, to set at liberty those who are oppressed; ¹⁹to proclaim the acceptable year of the Lord." (Luke 4:18–19)

And quite possibly, he was acting upon the declaration about the Messiah found in Psalm 72:12, which promises, "For He will deliver the needy when he cries, the poor also, and him who has no helper."

Calling Jesus the Son of David was a clear expression that this man believed He was the Messiah, and in a very real sense, it was also an expression of His faith in the promises about the Messiah.

He Cried Out All the More

When the blind man realized that it was Jesus passing by, he began to cry out. There was nothing polite or reserved about what he did. The Greek word translated *cried* literally means "to shout or scream for help in a tumultuous way."

When he was told to be quiet, he cried out all the more, or as the Amplified Bible, Classic Edition puts it, *"He screamed and shrieked so much the more"* (v. 39). He was not going to let his opportunity pass by.

Many people would never dream of desperately, publicly crying out to God for help. And I suspect that the main reason would not be because they wouldn't want to disturb people, but rather because they would be too worried about what people would think of them.

Pride is a terrible thing, and the worst place to have your peace is in someone else's head. Pride is not compatible with faith. Pride is a robber. Pride will block the answers to your prayers. "God resists the proud but gives grace to the humble" (1 Peter 5:5). As we humble ourselves in the sight of the Lord, He will lift us up (James 4:10).

What Do You Want Me to Do for You?

After Jesus had them bring the man to Him, He asked him a seemingly ridiculous question, *"What do you want Me to do for you?"* Wasn't it obvious? Everyone there could see that he was blind. Why ask such a question at all? After all, He didn't ask the lepers that question when they cried out for mercy. What gives?

There are times when we must be specific in our prayers. God certainly sees our hearts, but He still wants us to be specific when we ask things of Him. It is more for our own benefit than anything else. So many times there are a range of different needs that come to mind and heart when we pray, but faith requires focus.

This man cried out for mercy, but that is actually a fairly broad request. The Scriptures refer to guidance, peace, material supply, healing, favor, strength, forgiveness, and a lot more as manifestations of God's mercy. This blind man was also poor, as he was a beggar. He had material needs. Did he have a family? Was he previously a skilled craftsman, a musician? Had he lost his sight in an accident and had he lost his home or family as a result?

We are not told, but any number of needs could have been vying for the attention of his heart like a bird flying against the bars of its cage, seeking escape. Jesus wanted him to be specific, and we should not hesitate to be specific when we articulate our requests to the Lord.

His request became laser sharp when he said, *"Lord, that I may receive my sight,"* and as with so many others, Jesus declared that faith was the avenue through which his miracle came.

He Followed

After he was healed, he didn't go his own way. He joined the procession of those who were following Jesus. He joyfully praised God for the mercy that was shown to him, and so did all the people.

In the Garden

We now move to the final act of healing recorded by Dr. Luke in his Gospel, and it is truly astonishing. Jesus is in the garden with his disciples. While He prays, they sleep. Suddenly the scene is broken when Judas arrives, bringing an armed crowd. He betrays Jesus with a kiss, and His enemies lay their hands on Him. Peter suddenly lashes out with a sword, cutting off the right ear of the servant of the high priest.

We read, "And one of them struck the servant of the high priest and cut off his right ear. But Jesus answered and said, 'Permit even this.' And He touched his ear and healed him" (Luke 22:50–51).

What Jesus said can be looked at two ways. First, His words were likely addressed to His disciples, telling them to allow His unlawful arrest, for it was necessary to fulfill the plan of God. Secondly, it is quite possible that His words were addressed to His enemies. According to Matthew's account, the mob had already laid hands on Jesus, and He may have been speaking to them to permit Him to heal the man's severed ear.

However one looks at it, it is still amazing that even as Jesus is betrayed by one of His own and arrested by an angry mob, He is still healing! And think of the enormous compassion and undeserved mercy that was displayed to this man who had lost his ear.

He had come to do Jesus harm, but Jesus only did him good. Dear friend, it is the Lord's will to heal. To see Jesus is to see the Father. He is the will of God in action. He has not changed. He is still the same compassionate Healer today, and blessed are all those who put their trust in Him.

Part Two

THE BOOK OF ACTS

Both the Gospel of Luke and the book of Acts were written by Luke the beloved physician. In fact, they are both addressed to a man named Theophilus. As the book of Acts opens, it says, "The former account I made, O Theophilus, of all that Jesus began both to do and teach." The *former account* he is referring to is the Gospel of Luke. The gospel account tells about what Jesus *began* to do and teach. The book of Acts tells of what Jesus *continued* to do and teach through the Church via the Holy Spirit, who was sent back to empower us and guide us. So, as we dive into the book of Acts, we will be witnessing the continued ministry of Jesus Christ through His Church. And as we shall see, healing still continues to be a top priority with the Lord. And it is good to remember that the book of Acts is not just a historical account of what happened in and through the early church. In many ways it serves as a blueprint for the Church and its activity in every generation.

CHAPTER

13

The Lord's Continued Ministry Through His Church

Luke tells us that just before He ascended into heaven, the Lord left the disciples with this message: "Behold, I send the Promise of My Father upon you; but tarry in the city of Jerusalem until you are endued with power from on high" (Luke 24:49). As the book of Acts opens up, we are greeted with this same scene with a bit more detail added.

> [4]And being assembled together with them, He commanded them not to depart from Jerusalem, but to wait for the Promise of the Father, "which," He said, "you have heard from Me; [5]for John truly baptized with water, but you shall be baptized with the Holy Spirit not many days from now." . . . [8]But you shall receive power when the Holy Spirit has come upon you; and you shall be witnesses to Me in Jerusalem, and in all Judea and Samaria, and to the end of the earth." (Acts 1:4–5, 8)

Both in the gospel account and here in Acts, Jesus emphatically told them that they would *receive* or *be endued* (literally "be clothed") with *power* when they were baptized with the Holy Spirit. The Greek word *dunamis* translated as "power" in these verses could be rendered "miracle-working power." It is actually translated as the word "miracle" in the New Testament no less than eight times and is used more than thirty times in connection with miraculous physical healing.

For example, it is the word translated *power* in Luke 6:19 where it says, "And the whole multitude sought to touch Him, for power went out from Him and healed them all."

Similarly, when Jesus perceived that *power* went out from Him, healing the woman who had a flow of blood for twelve years, the same word is used (Luke 8:46). Luke uses the word again in Acts 10:38 where he declares, "How God anointed Jesus of Nazareth with the Holy Spirit and with power, who went about doing good and healing all who were oppressed by the devil, for God was with Him."

Though that power can also accomplish other things, it is what brought about the miraculous healings in the ministry of Jesus before His ascension, and now, as we journey through the book of Acts together, we will see this same power in operation as the Holy Spirit works through the Church.

If you want to do a bit of personal meditation and study along these lines, here is a partial list of verses where Luke uses the word *dunamis*: Luke 4:36; 5:17; 6:19; 8:46; 9:1; 10:19; 19:37; 24:49; Acts 2:22; 3:12; 4:7, 33; 6:8; 8:13; 19:11.

Baptized with the Holy Spirit and the Healings Begin

In Acts 2, as 120 were gathered together praying, there was a mighty outpouring of the Spirit, and they were all filled (baptized) with the Spirit and began to speak with other tongues.

Then Peter preached a simple message about Christ to the amazed multitudes that were witnessing what was going on. The result was that thousands put their trust in Jesus. And shortly after that, some notable healing miracles began to occur.

When Peter finished his sermon to the multitude after the coming of the Holy Spirit, we read,

> ^{41}Then those who gladly received his word were baptized; and that day about three thousand souls were added to them. ^{42}And they continued steadfastly in the apostles' doctrine and fellowship, in the breaking of bread, and in prayers. ^{43}Then fear came upon every soul, and many wonders and signs were done through the apostles. ^{44}Now all who believed were together, and had all things in common, ^{45}and sold their possessions and goods, and divided them among all, as anyone had need.
>
> ^{46}So continuing daily with one accord in the temple, and breaking bread from house to house, they ate their food with gladness and simplicity of heart, ^{47}praising God and having favor with all the people. And the Lord added to the church daily those who were being saved. (Acts 2:41–47)

From these verses, we get a clear picture of the infant Church. As we examine them, we can see some key elements that should be found in the Church in each successive generation. It is a blueprint of sorts for the Church in every generation. The following is a list of the things we immediately learn about the early church.

1. **It was a soul-winning Church.** That day, 3,000 souls were added! Oswald Chambers said that the Church that doesn't evangelize will fossilize. I believe that is true. Our number-one mission as believers is to share the good news and win others to Christ.

2. **It was a learning Church.** They continued steadfastly in the apostles' doctrine. Jesus said in John 8:31–32, "If you abide in My word, you are My disciples indeed. And you shall know the truth, and the truth shall make you free."

Feeding upon God's Word is the single most important element to spiritual growth and development. Think about it: they have just experienced a miraculous outpouring of the Spirit to the point that some onlookers even thought they must be drunk, but the apostles were not content to just experience the manifestations of the Spirit. They wanted to get the new believers grounded in good teaching.

Some groups and individuals today seem to want all Spirit and very little teaching. Or they may accentuate worship, which in itself is a very good thing, but not at the expense of failing to educate people's souls.

The Word must be taught to God's people, otherwise we will end up with believers who are *a mile wide and an inch deep.* If we do not provide a steady diet of the milk and meat of the Word, our churches will be shallow in their understanding and proclamation of the gospel and our worship will be shallow as well.

3. **It was a Church of fellowship.** They also continued steadfastly in fellowship and the breaking of bread (partaking of the Lord's

Supper and sharing meals). The old saying that *no man is an island* is true. God has created us for fellowship.

Ephesians 4:16 tells us that the body grows by every part doing its share and by supplying what God has placed within them to give. We need what other members in the body supply. No one person can do everything or be everything. God has made it so that we are dependent on community.

4. **It was a prayerful Church.** They continued steadfastly in prayers as well. They had regular prayer times that they observed. They went *in* to God before they went *out* into the world. They were able to meet the problems of life because they had first met with Him.

5. **It was a reverent Church.** The Scripture tells us that *fear* came upon every soul. That means that they had a genuine sense of awe and holy respect for God and for the things of God.

6. **It was a supernatural Church.** Many wonders and signs were done through the apostles. And though we read that miracles occurred through the apostles, as we progress in the book of Acts, we will soon find that they were not the only ones that God used. Jesus said that believers would do the same works that He did and greater because He was going to the Father and would send back the Holy Spirit (John 14:12–18).

7. **It was a generous Church.** Apparently their extravagant giving was spontaneous. It seems to have been born of their zeal and Spirit-inspired love for one another but was in no way mandatory.

8. **It was both a large and a small Church.** They met in large gatherings in the temple and in small gatherings from house to house.

9. **It was a worshiping Church.** They *praised* God and had favor with all the people.

Though every one of these aspects of the Church is important and an entire book could be written about each facet that was mentioned, we will continue to concentrate on the supernatural element that was so profoundly a part of the early church and the Lord's ministry through her.

CHAPTER
14

Captivated by the Supernatural

We read that *many* signs and wonders were done through the apostles. In fact, it was almost immediately following Peter's sermon on the day of Pentecost that a notable healing miracle occurred.

The Beautiful Gate

¹Now Peter and John went up together to the temple at the hour of prayer, the ninth hour. ²And a certain man lame from his mother's womb was carried, whom they laid daily at the gate of the temple which is called Beautiful, to ask alms from those who entered the temple; ³who, seeing Peter and John about to go into the temple, asked for alms. ⁴And fixing his eyes on him, with John, Peter said, "Look at us." ⁵So he gave them his attention, expecting to receive something from them. ⁶Then Peter said, "Silver and gold I do not have, but what I do have I give you: In the name of Jesus Christ of Nazareth, rise up and walk." ⁷And he took

him by the right hand and lifted him up, and immediately his feet and ankle bones received strength. ⁸So he, leaping up, stood and walked and entered the temple with them—walking, leaping, and praising God. ⁹And all the people saw him walking and praising God. ¹⁰Then they knew that it was he who sat begging alms at the Beautiful Gate of the temple; and they were filled with wonder and amazement at what had happened to him. (Acts 3:1–10)

The Jews had three set times for prayer. Peter and John were on their way to the temple at the 3 o'clock hour of prayer. As they were about to go into the temple, they crossed paths with a lame beggar. The beggar's life would be forever changed after this encounter and it would serve as a catalyst for the gospel to be proclaimed, for a time of unified prayer by the Church, and for the name of Jesus to be magnified.

This lame man was laid daily at what was referred to as the *Beautiful* Gate of the temple. According to Josephus, this Beautiful Gate was made of Corinthian brass whose exquisite workmanship far exceeded that of the other gates that were plated with gold and silver. It was so massive that it took the strength of twenty men to open and shut it. But beauty alone cannot relieve the suffering of those who are afflicted with sickness and disease.

You can have a wealthy church with ornate carvings on every wall and a million-dollar pipe organ, yet that church may be utterly bankrupt of spiritual power, while down the street is a little church in a rented storefront where the power of the Spirit is in manifestation.

Jesus Himself would have entered through this gate many times. If the lame beggar was laid daily at that gate, Jesus, no doubt, passed the man by, leaving him in his condition. Who knows, but Jesus may have even put some coins in the man's dish a time or two.

Along with this particular lame man, Jesus would have also seen many other lame people during the years of His ministry, but as this man clearly demonstrates, all sick or handicapped people were not healed under the ministry of Jesus. (Please reread chapter 1 for some more extensive teaching on why this was true.)

A careful reading of the Gospels will reveal an interesting truth: *Jesus did not heal all the sick people He came to, but He did heal all the sick people who came to Him.* In the case of the lame man who was healed in Acts 3, was his healing a matter of divine timing? Is that why Jesus had previously passed him by? Perhaps. It may also have had to do with the man's own state of mind.

Like everyone else in Jerusalem, he would have heard about Jesus. He would have heard the stories of the miraculous healings He had performed on the blind, the lame, and the lepers. He would have been alerted when Jesus was nearby because of the crowds and commotion that often surrounded Him.

Yet this lame man never cried out like blind Bartimaeus or struggled to get to Jesus like the woman with the flow of blood. He never asked any friends to carry him to Jesus like the paralyzed man whose friends tore the roof off. Since there were people who *daily* carried him and laid him at the gate (and no doubt also daily carried him home), could he not have persuaded them to carry him to Jesus, as Christ sat on the mountain and healed the multitudes? Others brought (and in some cases carried) the lame, blind, and maimed and laid them at Jesus' feet. And all who did so were healed (Matthew 15:29–31).

I can still remember asking a Christian friend to come with me to a meeting being held in a local hall by a traveling evangelist. I shared with her how people were giving their hearts to Jesus at the meetings and how some amazing healings were taking place. My friend had a serious health problem that could not be cured medically.

"Come and let the evangelist pray for you," I pleaded. "God is doing something special in these meetings. I know some of the people that have been healed. Please come." But she was not interested. The truth was she had given up on ever being healed. She was in a slow downward spiral physically and she had grown accustomed to it.

Dear reader, if this describes you, I want to encourage you to not lose hope. Keep expecting. Keep looking up. Psalm 27:13 says, "I would have lost heart, unless I had believed that I would see the goodness of the Lord in the land of the living."

It seems, from the little we are told about him, that the lame man at the Beautiful Gate had ceased looking up (or having any hope of being healed) a long time ago. He was so locked into his rut and routine that he was not even *really* looking at the people from whom he was asking money. Peter emphatically told him, "*Look at us.*" So he gave them his attention (something he had not been doing before), expecting to receive something from them. He was expecting a handout, but he was about to receive much more.

What I Do Have

After getting the man's full attention, Peter told him that he didn't *have* any silver or gold, which in Greek means that he didn't have any money *on hand*. After all, they were on their way to a prayer meeting. There was no need to carry a bag of coins with them into the temple. And they did have material resources, for Acts 2:44–45 tells us that the new believers had been selling their possessions and goods in order to provide for anyone who had need.

Then Peter told the man, "But what I do have I give you" (Acts 3:6). A different Greek word is used for *have* in this statement. It means "to possess." It is something that I have with me at all times. What was it that Peter possessed? It was the authority of the name of Jesus!

Peter then commanded the man to rise up and walk in the name of Jesus, and a startling miracle of healing occurred. And true to form, Dr. Luke uses medical terms to describe things. In his exposition of the book of Acts, G. Campbell Morgan explains this superbly, so I have included his words in their completeness here.

> Observe carefully the particular words made use of in the story of his healing: "Immediately his feet and his ankle-bones received strength. And leaping up, he stood, and began to walk." Perhaps only medical men can fully appreciate the meaning of these words; they are the peculiar, technical words of a medical man. The word translated feet, is only used by Luke, and occurs nowhere else. It indicates his discrimination between different parts of the human foot. This particular word refers to the base, or heel. The phrase ankle-bones is again a medical phrase, to be found nowhere else. The word "leaping up" describes the coming suddenly into socket of something that was out of place, the articulation of a joint. This then is a very careful medical description of what happened in connection with this man.[1]

What an amazing scene. The previously lame-from-birth beggar is now walking, leaping, and praising God. Everyone in the temple area knew him and they were awestruck at what had occurred.

> [11]Now as the lame man who was healed held on to Peter and John, all the people ran together to them in the porch which is called Solomon's, greatly amazed. [12]So when Peter saw it, he responded to the people: "Men of Israel, why do you marvel at this? Or why look so intently at us, as

though by our own power or godliness we had made this man walk? ¹³The God of Abraham, Isaac, and Jacob, the God of our fathers, glorified His Servant Jesus, whom you delivered up and denied in the presence of Pilate, when he was determined to let Him go. ¹⁴But you denied the Holy One and the Just, and asked for a murderer to be granted to you, ¹⁵and killed the Prince of life, whom God raised from the dead, of which we are witnesses. ¹⁶And His name, through faith in His name, has made this man strong, whom you see and know. Yes, the faith which comes through Him has given him this perfect soundness in the presence of you all." (Acts 3:11–16)

Peter made it clear that the miracle could not be attributed to his personal holiness or to some power that he had in and of himself. He immediately pointed that awestruck crowd to Jesus. And he said that it was through faith in the name of Jesus that healing and soundness had been brought to the man.

Like all believers, Peter had been given the privilege and responsibility to use that matchless name. In the next chapter in Acts, when the Sanhedrin asked Peter, "By what power or by what name have you done this?" Peter boldly declares that it was by the name of Jesus Christ of Nazareth and that His name has been given to men (Acts 4:7–12).

All Authority

Both Matthew and Mark share different aspects of what is commonly referred to as *the Great Commission*, which refers to the final instructions that Jesus issued to His disciples, and subsequently to His Church in every generation, just before He ascended into heaven. When we put the two accounts together we discover something very powerful—something that Peter knew and put to work that day at the Beautiful Gate.

Matthew 28:18–20 says,

> ¹⁸And Jesus came and spoke to them, saying, "*All authority has been given to Me in heaven and on earth.* ¹⁹*Go therefore* and make disciples of all the nations, baptizing them in the name of the Father and of the Son and of the Holy Spirit, ²⁰teaching them to observe all things that I have commanded you; and lo, I am with you always, even to the end of the age." Amen. (emphasis mine)

As soon as Jesus declared that all authority in heaven and on earth was His, He said, "**Go therefore**," make disciples, baptize, and teach. He is clearly *delegating* His authority to His followers.

Mark records these details about the same event:

> ¹⁵And He said to them, "Go into all the world and preach the gospel to every creature. ¹⁶He who believes and is baptized will be saved; but he who does not believe will be condemned. ¹⁷And these signs will follow those who believe: **In My name** they will cast out demons; they will speak with new tongues; ¹⁸they will take up serpents; and if they drink anything deadly, it will by no means hurt them; they will lay hands on the sick, and they will recover." (Mark 16:15–18, emphasis mine)

Like Matthew, Mark is clear about our Lord's command to go into all the nations with the gospel. Matthew shows us that we are commissioned to carry His delegated authority as we carry out the mission, and Mark makes it clear that that authority is to be exercised by all believers ***in His name***!

They Locked Her Up Every Night

As a young believer, I spent some time in Mexico helping with a gospel crusade. The event was being held in a crude soccer field that had been dug out of the side of a cliff in a hilly area above the town of Ensenada in Baja California.

Part of what I did, for several days before and during the event, was drive around the dirt roads of the little villages in the region passing out flyers for the crusade as well as advertising the event with a bullhorn through the window of my old Volkswagen bus.

One afternoon a woman (we will call her Martha) stood in the middle of one of those dirt roads, frantically waving her arms. She refused to let us pass. After I stopped and got out, Martha insisted that I and the people with me come into her home and pray for her.

It seems that her aunt was a local *bruja,* or witch. She went on to tell us how her aunt had cast a spell on her several years ago and ever since, whenever the sun would set, Martha would lose her mind.

Her father lived with her and her children in that humble, tiny house. Every night he would lock Martha in a cellar just a little while before sunset because once the sun would set she would become like a wild animal, lashing out at everyone and everything, and on several occasions she had even tried to kill her own children.

Once the sun would rise, she would have no memory of the night before. Her father would unlock the chain on the cellar door and she would come out exhausted but ready to face another day. That had been her life for several years!

We laid our hands on her head and earnestly prayed. Using the name of Jesus, we commanded the tormenting spirit to leave her and her family. Nothing visibly took place, but we were confident that the evil spirit had been dealt with. The next night Martha was at the crusade with her children! She had been set free.

She came early every night, children in tow, and would get a seat as close to the front as she could. When the worship portion of the services took place it was amazing to watch Martha with her hands raised, praising and thanking God. What set her free? What restored her right mind to her? It was the authority of the name of Jesus!

Through Faith in His Name

All authority in heaven and earth belongs to Jesus. He has delegated that authority to His Church. We exercise that authority by using the name of Jesus. Yet there is something that must work in conjunction with that. *It is faith.*

Peter said it was the name of Jesus that made the lame man whole, but he also said that it was His name *through faith in His name* (Acts 3:16). Mark told us that the signs of healing and casting out demons would be done in the name of Jesus, but he also said they would follow those *who believe* (Mark 16:17).

There is power in His name, but as far as Christians using that name, faith is required to unlock its potential. How does one acquire faith in that name? Romans 10:17 declares, "So then faith comes by hearing, and hearing by the word of God."

A prayerful study of the New Testament about the name of Jesus will yield much fruit. Take the time to look up and ponder every place it is spoken of in the Gospels and in the epistles. As you do, faith will come unconsciously, and faith in His name can do astonishing things.

Wonder and Amazement

"If I could just see a miracle I would have faith," some people say. What was the response of the people who saw the man who had been lame from birth when he was miraculously healed? The Scripture says that they were filled with wonder and amazement—*not faith*.

For those who say they would believe if they saw a miracle, the truth is that they would likely be amazed, but they would not be suddenly filled with faith. Faith comes by hearing God's Word. That's why once the crowd of greatly amazed people gathered, Peter began to preach to them about Jesus. That is the same thing he did in Acts 2 when the crowd gathered after the outpouring of the Spirit in the upper room.

Neither speaking in tongues nor miracles (as marvelous as those things are) will save people. They may arrest people's attention, but God has chosen to save those who believe through the foolishness of the message preached (1 Corinthians 1:21). Speaking of the events of this man's healing and Peter following it up by preaching to the crowd about Jesus and the resurrection, the Scriptures declare that many of them *who heard the word* believed (Acts 4:4).

Her World Was Falling Apart

I was serving as an assistant pastor in a small church when Janet and I married in 1982. We were living in a small apartment at the far end of town. Living in the apartment right next to ours was a woman (whom we will call Gloria) and her boyfriend (whom we will call Juan).

One day Gloria knocked at our door asking to use our phone (this was long before mobile phones were invented). Opening the door, I said, "Sure, it's on the wall in the kitchen." It seemed like it took her ten minutes to move from the door to the kitchen about fifteen feet away. She was a young woman and it was surprising to see her in such terrible pain. Every step was agonizing for her.

"What's wrong?" I asked. "Oh, I injured my back," she responded. After making her call, she made the painful trek back to our front door and on to her apartment.

After Gloria left, I felt very convicted in my heart. I was a pastor. I taught on the subject of healing, I prayed for the sick, and here was my neighbor in extreme pain in my apartment and I didn't even offer to pray for her. I decided right then what I would do. I walked next door and knocked on her apartment door. It seemed like it took ages for her to answer the door.

When she opened the door, I said, "Gloria, I need to tell you something. My wife and I are Christians and the Bible teaches that Jesus is a healer." I shared with her from Mark 16:18 where Jesus said that believers would lay hands on the sick and they would recover.

When I told her that she began to sob. She told me that she was in terrific pain and that she didn't know what had happened to her boyfriend Juan. He had gone to Mexico and was supposed to return in two days, but it had been two weeks and she hadn't heard a word. "I don't know what I'm going to do," she said as tears streamed down her face.

Now I was really convicted. Here was my neighbor, literally living on the other side of the wall from us, and her whole world was falling apart, and I had no idea it was going on. I felt like a man who had plenty of bread, yet there were starving people a few feet away and I had been oblivious to it!

With her permission I laid my hands on her head and prayed for her healing. I also prayed that God would keep Juan safe and that she would hear from him soon. She thanked me and hobbled painfully back to a chair. Nothing discernible had occurred, at least not yet . . .

The next day, Gloria was at our door, knocking away. When I answered it, she had a huge smile on her face. "Juan got in touch with me this morning through a friend. He's on his way home! And look!" she exclaimed. Then she started bending over again and again. "All of the pain is gone. I'm healed!"

Then something really unexpected happened. She asked, "Will you come over to my place and tell me more about Jesus?" "Sure," I said as I scooped up my Bible. Over the next half hour, I sat across from Gloria at her coffee table, reading her Scriptures and explaining the plan of salvation. When I finished she took my hand and prayed with me, giving her heart to the Lord. It was glorious!

Gloria's conversion story wasn't too different than the multitude we read about that observed the healing of the lame man at the Beautiful Gate. The supernatural arrested their attention, but they had to hear the Word preached in order to be saved (Acts 4:4).

CHAPTER

15

Resistance from the Sadducees

The Same Sun That Melts Butter Hardens Clay

As we come to the next part of Dr. Luke's narrative, we quickly find that not everyone was happy about the lame man's miraculous healing or about the apostles' preaching.

> ¹Now as they spoke to the people, the priests, the captain of the temple, and the Sadducees came upon them, ²being greatly disturbed that they taught the people and preached in Jesus the resurrection from the dead. ³And they laid hands on them, and put them in custody until the next day, for it was already evening. ⁴However, many of those who heard the word believed; and the number of the men came to be about five thousand. (Acts 4:1–4)

The Sadducees were made up of many aristocratic, wealthy Jews. They believed in God and in the law of Moses, but they denied the supernatural. They didn't believe in angels or in the resurrection (Acts 23:8; Matthew 22:23).

Yet here they are, confronted by an undeniable miracle of healing. It flew in the face of what they claimed to be non-existent. Are they happy? Far from it. They were greatly disturbed by the miracle and by the apostles preaching about the resurrection. Yet as they hardened their hearts in unbelief, multitudes of others believed.

The same sun that melts butter hardens clay. Witnessing the miraculous and hearing the gospel will melt some hearts, resulting in their conversion, while it will harden other hearts, resulting in their damnation. It all depends on the posture of heart we choose to take.

> [5]And it came to pass, on the next day, that their rulers, elders, and scribes, [6]as well as Annas the high priest, Caiaphas, John, and Alexander, and as many as were of the family of the high priest, were gathered together at Jerusalem. [7]And when they had set them in the midst, they asked, "By what power or by what name have you done this?" [8]Then Peter, filled with the Holy Spirit, said to them, "Rulers of the people and elders of Israel: [9]If we this day are judged for a good deed done to a helpless man, by what means he has been made well, [10]let it be known to you all, and to all the people of Israel, that by the name of Jesus Christ of Nazareth, whom you crucified, whom God raised from the dead, by Him this man stands here before you whole. [11]This is the 'stone which was rejected by you builders, which has become the chief cornerstone.' [12]Nor is there salvation in any other, for there is no other name under heaven given among men by which we must be saved." (Acts 4:5–12)

This crowd of religious elite represented the wealthiest, most intellectual, and most powerful people in the nation. They are the same ones who had condemned Jesus.

After spending the night under arrest, Peter and John are set in the midst before this sneering, indignant crowd. Most people would have been terrified and intimidated. In fact, not too many days past, Peter and the other disciples were hiding behind closed doors for fear of the Jews (John 20:19). But now, as the most influential men in Jerusalem oppose and question them, Peter is as bold as a lion.

What made the difference? The Holy Spirit!

Jesus had commanded the disciples to not depart from Jerusalem until they had received the promised infilling of the Holy Spirit. Once they had received the Spirit and began to speak in other tongues, they got out from behind their closed doors and began preaching boldly in the street (Acts 1:4–8; 2:1–41).

And now again, as Peter stands before the Sanhedrin, it is stated that he was filled with the Holy Spirit. Instead of withering because of intimidation, he addressed them boldly and confidently. When they put the same question to the apostles that they had put to Jesus in Matthew 21:23, Peter was not shy about giving them an answer.

A Good Deed

Peter begins by calling the man's healing good. In Acts 10:38, it says that Jesus "went about *doing good* and healing." Healing and health are good. Sickness is bad. As rudimentary as that is, it is surprising how many religious people get it wrong.

They (like the Pharisees wanted to do) are quick to attribute miraculous power to the devil while telling people that God is the one who made them sick. That is the exact opposite of what the Scriptures teach.

God is good. Healing is good. The devil is the one who kills, steals, and destroys (John 10:10).

In addressing the crowd, Peter is clear that the man's healing should be attributed to God and that it was done in the name of Jesus Christ of Nazareth—the very One whom those assembled had condemned and crucified, who had now been raised from the dead.

It is also noteworthy that when Peter talks about the man being made well (or healed) in verse 9, he uses the Greek word *sozo*. It is a common word used in the New Testament for healing, but it is also the word used for salvation. As he continues to talk about the man's healing, Peter uses the word again in verse 12 when he says, "There is no other name under heaven given among men, whereby we must be *saved*" (emphasis mine).

That is significant, for Peter was not speaking about the forgiveness of sins. The subject under discussion was healing! That means that Peter literally said (and that is how it would have been understood by those listening), "Nor is there healing in any other, for there is no other name under heaven given among men, whereby we must be ***healed***!"

There is healing in the name of Jesus, and healing is a part of salvation!

The Finishing Hammer

I once heard the story of a guy whose wife had given him a small finishing hammer as a birthday gift. It appeared to be well made, and he promptly put it in a kitchen drawer so it would be ready to use for any small household fix-it job. A few days later, he needed a screwdriver to take care of something but couldn't find one.

"Honey," he called out to his wife, "do you know where the screwdriver is?" "It's in the kitchen drawer," she said. He looked and looked but couldn't find a screwdriver in the drawer. "There isn't one there," he said. "Oh yes there is. I'll show you," she said with a smile.

She reached into the drawer and pulled out his new finishing hammer and handed it to him. "Here you go," she said. "Dear," he responded with a grin on his face, "that is not a screwdriver." "That's what you think," she said.

She then unscrewed the handle, revealing a solid-looking screwdriver inside. It had a reversible tip that could be used for different types of screws. "That's not all," she said as she unscrewed the end plate. Once it came off, she pushed a button and a powerful flashlight flared to life. "Now that's a surprise," he said. "I had no idea that it had more than one function."

That illustrates many people's viewpoint of salvation. In their minds, it only has to do with the forgiveness of sins, and while that is certainly a main part of salvation, God's idea of salvation is far broader than most people have realized.

This can be illustrated by the way Dr. Luke, inspired by the Holy Spirit, uses the Greek word *sozo*. We clearly saw that from Acts 4:9–12, but there is another section of Luke's writings that perhaps displays this same truth even better. It is found throughout Luke 8.

> "Those by the wayside are the ones who hear; then the devil comes and takes away the word out of their hearts, lest they should believe and be saved." (Luke 8:12)

In this verse, the word translated "saved" is *sozo*, referring to a person having a right relationship with God through faith.

> "They also who had seen it told them by what means he who had been demon-possessed was healed." (Luke 8:36)

In this verse, the word translated "healed" is *sozo*, referring to the man who was set free from demonic possession and having his right mind restored to him.

> "And He said to her, 'Daughter, be of good cheer; your faith has made you well. Go in peace.'" (Luke 8:48)

In this verse, the phrase translated "made you well" is *sozo*, referring to the physical healing of the woman's body.

> "But when Jesus heard it, He answered him, saying, 'Do not be afraid; only believe, and she will be made well.'" (Luke 8:50)

In this verse, the phrase translated "made well" is *sozo*, referring to the little girl who was to be raised from the dead.

God's Idea of Salvation

We can see from the Holy Spirit's use of the word salvation (*sozo*) in these verses in Luke 8 that God's idea of salvation encompasses much more than most people recognize. Just like there were more functions to the finishing hammer that the wife gave to her husband, the salvation that Christ came and purchased for us includes several things.

It deals with sin and brings us into a relationship with God. It provides peace and soundness for our minds, freeing us from the enemy's oppression. It provides healing for our bodies, and ultimately, it rescues us from death itself through the resurrection.

That It Spreads No Further

> [13]Now when they saw the boldness of Peter and John, and perceived that they were uneducated and untrained men, they marveled. And they realized that they had been with

Jesus. ¹⁴And seeing the man who had been healed standing with them, they could say nothing against it. ¹⁵But when they had commanded them to go aside out of the council, they conferred among themselves, ¹⁶saying, "What shall we do to these men? For, indeed, that a notable miracle has been done through them is evident to all who dwell in Jerusalem, and we cannot deny it. ¹⁷But so that it spreads no further among the people, let us severely threaten them, that from now on they speak to no man in this name." (Acts 4:13–17)

When the Sadducees asked Peter, "By what power or by what name have you done this?" he responded by quoting Psalm 118:22, basically telling them that they had fulfilled it. What gave this even more impact is that it was the very verse that Jesus quoted to them when they asked Him the same question (Acts 4:7, 11; Matthew 21:23–42).

No wonder they realized that these men had been with Jesus. They were bold like He was and they talked just like Him!

Being surprised at the boldness of Peter and John, coupled with the fact that the lame man who was now healed was standing with them, these religious leaders realized that they couldn't harm them (though they obviously wanted to). Conferring among themselves, they decided to severely threaten them before letting them go.

They wanted to put a stop to the gathering momentum. In fact, what they said among themselves was shocking: "So that it spreads no further among the people." So that no more helpless people would be healed, so that no one else would put their trust in Jesus, they commanded them to speak no more to any man in the name of Jesus.

Think of it! Every member of the Sanhedrin would have been aware of the paralyzed man and his condition. They knew how miserable his life had been. And now, he stands before them absolutely whole.

Instead of begging for scraps, he can now work. He can take care of a family. Instead of lameness, he is leaping and praising God. And the religious leaders don't want it to spread. They don't want any more good news or good deeds of healing to touch people in need. They don't want a risen Savior in their lives and they don't want anyone else to find out about Him.

Working through these wicked men was the devil, who will do anything he can to silence the gospel. If the gospel is not preached, if Jesus is not proclaimed, then the light will not come and men and women will remain under the control of darkness.

First Corinthians 1:18 declares, "For the message of the cross is foolishness to those who are perishing, but to us who are being saved it is the power of God." (The Greek word translated "saved" in this verse is *sozo*.)

Romans 1:16 says, "For I am not ashamed of the gospel of Christ, for it is the power of God to salvation for everyone who believes, for the Jew first and also for the Greek." The gospel brings the power of God to forgive sin, give peace, and provide healing. When we hear it proclaimed boldly and in its fullness (not watered down), it produces faith to procure all of these things. It is what God wants, and it is what the devil fears most.

Where Silent People Come and Go

When it comes to churches, Satan doesn't care if we are a close-knit, caring community, as long as we are not actively engaged in proclaiming the gospel. Churches are not supposed to be like libraries where silent people come and go, most of the community not even being aware of their existence.

We are called to make a difference in the world, and while part of that difference is made through helping the poor and doing good works, far and away the biggest impact comes through the proclamation of the truth.

Speaking through the Sanhedrin, Satan attempted to muzzle the church in Jerusalem through threats and intimidation, but the disciples wouldn't have any of it! After calling them back in, the Jewish council commanded Peter and John not to speak at all or teach in the name of Jesus.

But Peter and John answered and said to them, "Whether it is right in the sight of God to listen to you more than God, you judge. For we cannot but speak the things which we have seen and heard" (Acts 4:19–20).

As the people of God, we are called to obey the governing authorities unless they bid us to disobey God or our conscience. There is a higher authority and rule that we owe our allegiance to. As Peter so aptly put it to the council just a short time later, "We ought to obey God rather than men" (Acts 5:29; 23:1).

Lord, Give Us More

After being released, Peter and John returned to their companions and reported all that the chief priests and elders had said to them. They made it clear to all that they had been severely threatened and told not to speak anymore in the name of Jesus.

Everyone present knew that these threats had been precipitated by the man's healing at the Beautiful Gate. In response to this news, they all began to pray. But what did they pray? *"Lord, help us to be compliant and to not stir up any trouble*"? No! In unison they prayed for boldness to speak God's Word and that *more* healings would occur in the name of Jesus (Acts 4:29–30). Or as Dr. Morgan puts it, "*They prayed for the continuance of that very activity which had produced the hostility.*"[1]

And God was not long in answering them:

> [31]And when they had prayed, the place where they were assembled together was shaken; and they were all filled with the Holy Spirit, and they spoke the word of God with boldness. . . . [33]And with great power the apostles gave witness to the resurrection of the Lord Jesus. And great grace was upon them all. (Acts 4:31, 33)

The Greek word translated as "power" in verse 33 is *dunamis*. It is the same word translated as "miracle" many places in the New Testament and is many times used directly in connection with divine healing.

For example, it is the word translated as "power" in Luke 6:19 where it says, "And the whole multitude sought to touch Him, for power went out from Him and healed them all." Through the miraculous healings that were taking place, the apostles were bearing witness to the resurrection of Jesus. After all, dead people can't heal anyone, but if people are being miraculously healed, that is a different story . . .

They Came Home Defeated

I had the privilege of knowing one of the (in my opinion) world's leading international evangelists. For over fifty years, he led healing evangelistic campaigns throughout the world, leading millions to Christ. In his later years, he would occasionally come and hold meetings at our church, which I cherished, not only for the impact of his ministry in our city but also for the meals and fellowship we had.

On one occasion, he told me how he and his wife went overseas to hold their first salvation campaign in a foreign country. He was preaching before a large crowd when he was challenged by a man in the audience.

"The things you are saying are not true and this Jesus you are talking about is not the Savior of the world!" the man yelled out. "The Bible disagrees with you, sir," the evangelist responded. "What is the Bible?" the man bellowed back. "It is the Word of God," he said.

"That is false too," the man said. "Your book is not the Word of God. Our book is God's word. Your book is false." The man then held up a copy of the book from his religion. The meeting was over. The crowd began to leave en masse. It was a region of the world dominated by another major world religion (with its own book of scripture).

My friend the evangelist, along with his wife, returned home defeated and discouraged. What could they do? How could they reach the hearts of these precious people steeped in and blinded by another religion?

They earnestly began to pray. A short time later, they found themselves in the meeting of another traveling evangelist here in the US. As they sat in that meeting, they were astounded because not only did the preacher bring a clear message of salvation and forgiveness, he also boldly prayed for the sick in the name of Jesus. And miracles were occurring! People were healed and multitudes put their trust in Christ as Savior.

"That's it!" my friend exclaimed to his wife. "When we return overseas, we must pray for the sick just like in the book of Acts. I believe that if we do, we will see multitudes come to Christ."

The following year, they returned to the very town where they had previously failed. Once again, they were challenged and were told that their message was false. "If our Jesus is alive and if He is the Son of God, He will heal people here today," the evangelist boldly proclaimed.

Then he called for any blind in the crowd to be brought forward. They brought a number of blind people forward and then he prayed for them. To the shock of the crowd, the blind began to see! It was a powerful witness to the resurrection and claims of Christ.

Most of the people in the meeting that day put their trust in Jesus. From that day forward, in more than seventy countries, over the next fifty years that man preached Christ and prayed for the sick. Miracles happened and before his race ended (both he and his wife have been in heaven for quite a few years now), millions were swept into the kingdom.

When the Church in Acts 4 prayed that God would grant them boldness to speak the Word and that He would stretch forth His hand to heal, the answer had an immediate effect, but it also carried on into the near future. We read in the very next chapter,

> [12]And through the hands of the apostles many signs and wonders were done among the people. And they were all with one accord in Solomon's Porch. [13]Yet none of the rest dared join them, but the people esteemed them highly. [14]And believers were increasingly added to the Lord, multitudes of both men and women, [15]so that they brought the sick out into the streets and laid them on beds and couches, that at least the shadow of Peter passing by might fall on some of them. [16]Also a multitude gathered from the surrounding cities to Jerusalem, bringing sick people and those who were tormented by unclean spirits, and they were all healed. (Acts 5:12–16)

Healing was and is a big part of God's agenda for His Church. Perhaps if we would lift our voices in unison today and pray for what they prayed for then, we might see some of the same results.

Four Distinct Parts to Their Prayer

The prayer that the Church prayed that day when they were being threatened by the Sanhedrin trying to intimidate them into silence is very illuminating. It had four distinct parts, and I would suggest that believers use it as a pattern today whenever they are facing any kind of trouble or persecution or any dark or threatening cloud hanging over their life.

1. They magnified God.

In Acts 4:24, they said, "Lord, You are God, who made heaven and earth and the sea, and all that is in them." They thought about and acknowledged how big God is. When we do that, it helps put things in perspective. All of our problems are pretty small when compared to the greatness of God.

2. They found Scripture that applied to their situation and incorporated it into their prayer.

In Acts 4:25–26 they said, "Who by the mouth of Your servant David have said: 'Why did the nations rage, and the people plot vain things? The kings of the earth took their stand, and the rulers were gathered together against the Lord and against His Christ.'"

They were quoting Psalm 2:1–2. They also knew that Psalm 2:4 said, "He who sits in the heavens shall laugh; the Lord shall hold them in derision."

It was a prophecy not only about the forces arrayed against Jesus at His arrest, trial, and crucifixion, it also speaks of the vain attempts of the Jewish and pagan powers to suppress Christianity.

In Acts 4:27, they prayed, "For truly against Your holy Servant Jesus, whom You anointed, both Herod and Pontius Pilate, with the Gentiles and the people of Israel, were gathered together."

A Jewish king, a Roman governor, the heathen (Gentiles), and the Jewish people all gathered together to oppose Christ and His kingdom. They were ungodly forces that normally were unfriendly to one another. It is worthy of note that groups that normally oppose one another may unite to oppose God and His purposes.

3. They realized that nothing takes God by surprise and that He always has a plan.

In verse 28 they said, "To do whatever Your hand and Your purpose determined before to be done." Has it ever occurred to you that nothing ever occurs to God? He is never caught off guard and He can make all things work together for our good. He sees you now. He is acquainted with your troubles and He made a way of escape before the trouble ever arrived (1 Corinthians 10:13; Romans 8:28).

4. They made a very specific request to God concerning their situation.

In verses 29–30 they said,

> ^{29}"Now, Lord, look on their threats, and grant to Your servants that with all boldness they may speak Your word, ^{30}by stretching out Your hand to heal, and that signs and wonders may be done through the name of Your holy Servant Jesus."

They didn't pray, "Look on their threats and smash them!" or "Look on their threats and keep us safe." They said, "Look on their threats and empower us!" Persecution shouldn't make us shrink, but rather, it should drive us to our knees to seek God for more boldness!

They prayed for boldness and for healing miracles to continue! It was the very thing they had been threatened not to do. They prayed for courage to do it more!

Also worth noting, they prayed about speaking the Word first (v. 29), and then they prayed for healing and miracles to occur. Why? Because faith comes by hearing the Word (Romans 10:17).

It was something they had learned from Jesus. His normal method of operation was to teach, preach, and *then* heal (Matthew 4:23; 9:35). They had learned it by observation as well as by precept, for Jesus had commanded them to preach first and then lay hands on the sick (Mark 16:15–20).

CHAPTER
16

Points to Ponder

Having come this far in Dr. Luke's account of healing in connection with the early church, here are a few points that I believe are worthy of some deeper consideration.

1. There will be resistance when we begin to boldly proclaim the gospel and pray for the sick to be healed.

We are swimming upstream in a downstream world. First John 5:19 says, "We know that we are of God, and the whole world lies under the sway of the wicked one." That being true, we also realize that when we engage in the God-ordained work of helping, healing, and bringing people into His kingdom, there will be resistance and persecution inspired by the enemy who wants to keep people in darkness and in bondage.

I Don't Want to See It and I Don't Want Anyone Else to See It

Though our outreach via television has grown into a global, multi-language work, it certainly didn't begin that way. Our beginnings were humble and quite small. My wife and I started doing a weekly half-hour show about biblical principles for marriage.

The shows were taped by volunteers in a little back alley, public access studio on antiquated equipment. Our show aired on that public access station one night a week at about 3 a.m. To our knowledge, no one ever even saw it except one local resident who went to the city council to have it removed. He basically said, "I don't want to see it and I don't want anyone else to see it either!"

It was ridiculous. Our show was literally on at 3 a.m. on a tiny station that almost no one knew existed. But it does illustrate the point well. We were talking about Jesus and the devil wasn't happy. It is easier to pull up a tree when it is a just-planted little sapling as opposed to once it has taken root and grown into a sturdy, fruit-bearing giant. Satan will always oppose the forward march of the gospel and all of the blessings it brings. We must not be taken by surprise when it happens.

We saw it take place through the Jewish council in Peter's day and it is still happening today. Resistance will come, but if we don't quit, we will win, and the message of our King and His kingdom will continue to go forth, liberating captives and bringing them into all of the benefits the Lord has provided through Calvary.

2. If we are going to be a powerful Church, we must have unity.

In reading about the man's healing at the Beautiful Gate and the events that surrounded it, one can hardly overlook the fact that the Church was unified. In Acts 1:14, it is declared about the disciples, "These all continued **with one accord** in prayer and supplication, with the women and Mary the mother of Jesus, and with His brothers" (emphasis mine).

Acts 2:1 says, "When the Day of Pentecost had fully come, they were all **_with one accord_** in one place" (emphasis mine). Verse 46 of the same chapter tells us, "So continuing daily **_with one accord_** in the temple, and breaking bread from house to house, they ate their food with gladness and simplicity of heart" (emphasis mine).

Acts 4:24 tells us that when the Church prayed, "they raised their voice to God **_in one accord_**" (emphasis mine).

Acts 4:32 declares, "Now the multitude of those who believed were of **_one heart and one soul_**" (emphasis mine).

It would be difficult to overstate the importance of unity. Psalm 133 captures some of the reasons why unity is so vital for us:

> ¹Behold, how good and how pleasant it is for brethren to dwell together in unity! ²It is like the precious oil upon the head, running down on the beard, the beard of Aaron, running down on the edge of his garments. ³It is like the dew of Hermon, descending upon the mountains of Zion; for there the Lord commanded the blessing—life forevermore.

This psalm tells us that dwelling in unity is good and pleasant (meaning that disunity is bad and unpleasant), and it is also like precious oil upon the head. This refers to the anointing of Aaron, the brother of Moses, who was the first high priest.

In this psalm, Aaron is a type of the Church and the oil is a type of the anointing and power of the Holy Spirit. When the Church is moving in unity, that anointing will affect every member of the body of Christ (running down to the very borders of the priest's garment). When brothers are in unity there will be refreshing (dew of Hermon) and the lost will be won to Christ (the blessing of life forevermore).

When talking to the Father near the end of His earthly ministry, Jesus prayed, "That they all may be one, as You, Father, are in Me, and I in You; that they also may be one in Us, that the world may believe that You sent Me" (John 17:21).

He Kept Taking His Coat Off

It is very interesting to note the word that Jesus used when He told His disciples to wait for the coming of the Holy Spirit. In Luke 24:49, it is recorded that Jesus told them, "Behold, I send the Promise of My Father upon you; but tarry in the city of Jerusalem until you are endued with power from on high."

The Greek word translated as *endued* in this verse literally means "to be clothed or to put on a garment."

Jesus was quite literally telling them that they would be clothed with a garment of power. It was obvious that such a garment had come upon them for there was power in Peter's preaching (and as others spoke the Word with boldness), as well as a mighty demonstration of healing power that brought soundness and wholeness to the sick. It is God's desire for the Church in every generation to be clothed with such a garment.

With that in mind, consider Paul's plea to the church in Corinth:

> [10]Now I plead with you, brethren, by the name of our Lord Jesus Christ, that you all speak the same thing, and that there be no divisions among you, but that you be perfectly joined together in the same mind and in the same judgment. [11]For it has been declared to me concerning you, my brethren, by those of Chloe's household, that there are contentions among you. [12]Now I say this, that each of you says, "I am of Paul," or "I am of Apollos," or "I am of Cephas," or "I am

of Christ." ¹³Is Christ divided? Was Paul crucified for you? Or were you baptized in the name of Paul? (1 Corinthians 1:10–13)

The Greek word translated *divisions* found in verse 10 literally means "to rend or tear." It is used in the New Testament of the curtain in the temple being torn and in several other places of making a tear in fabric.

The idea is that when the Church is in strife and disharmony, we tear off that garment of power. We are still God's children, but when we are in disharmony, we find ourselves in the midst of sighing, crying, dying humanity and we have no power to help them.

There is little power in the preaching, no conviction of sin, no miracles, no signs, no wonders, and little or no healing. And yes, God is the One who heals and saves, but He has chosen to use His Church as the instrument through which that occurs.

When he was a little boy, our youngest son, Spencer, hated to wear coats. It didn't matter if it was cold or raining, for some reason he just didn't like to have one on. Being dutiful parents we always made him put a coat on when he went out into cold or inclement weather, but generally, before he had gone twenty paces, he would shed that coat. We were always following him around, saying, "Spencer, put your coat on!"

I think our heavenly Father has the same problem with His children!

3. If we are going to be a powerful Church, we must have purity.

The Clogged Sink

I can still remember the first time I unclogged a sink at our house. The water was backed up and wasn't draining at all. I opened the sink and shoved a bent coat hanger down the pipe to see if I could snag anything (I'm sure there were better ways of doing this, but it was new territory for me).

I actually did snag something and pulled it out of the pipe and up through the drain. Oh my! When I saw the awful-looking gunk that had stopped up our sink, I felt like I needed to put on a hazmat suit! It was ugly and stinky, and I was so glad to get it out and dispose of it so the water could flow freely again.

In the same way that the accumulated gunk clogged up our sink, sin will clog up the flow of the Holy Spirit through His Church. If there is known sin in your life, confess it to God and repent! If we are going to be a Church of power, we must also be a Church of purity. When Satan couldn't squash the momentum of the Church with threats and persecution (in fact, the Church only grew in that environment), he tried a different tactic. When he couldn't crush the Church from the outside, he tried to corrupt it from the inside.

Woven into the middle of this divine explosion of healing and souls coming into the kingdom during those first days of the Church, we find a story that is at the same time intriguing and alarming. It is the sad tale of a couple who tried to lie to the Holy Spirit. Their names were Ananias and Sapphira:

> [34]Nor was there anyone among them who lacked; for all who were possessors of lands or houses sold them, and brought the proceeds of the things that were sold, [35]and laid them at the apostles' feet; and they distributed to each as anyone had need.
>
> [36]And Joses, who was also named Barnabas by the apostles (which is translated Son of Encouragement), a Levite of the

country of Cyprus, ³⁷having land, sold it, and brought the money and laid it at the apostles' feet.

¹But a certain man named Ananias, with Sapphira his wife, sold a possession. ²And he kept back part of the proceeds, his wife also being aware of it, and brought a certain part and laid it at the apostles' feet. ³But Peter said, "Ananias, why has Satan filled your heart to lie to the Holy Spirit and keep back part of the price of the land for yourself? ⁴While it remained, was it not your own? And after it was sold, was it not in your own control? Why have you conceived this thing in your heart? You have not lied to men but to God."

⁵Then Ananias, hearing these words, fell down and breathed his last. So great fear came upon all those who heard these things. ⁶And the young men arose and wrapped him up, carried him out, and buried him.

⁷Now it was about three hours later when his wife came in, not knowing what had happened. ⁸And Peter answered her, "Tell me whether you sold the land for so much?" She said, "Yes, for so much."

⁹Then Peter said to her, "How is it that you have agreed together to test the Spirit of the Lord? Look, the feet of those who have buried your husband are at the door, and they will carry you out." ¹⁰Then immediately she fell down at his feet and breathed her last. And the young men came in and found her dead, and carrying her out, buried her by her husband. ¹¹So great fear came upon all the church and upon all who heard these things. (Acts 4:34–5:11)

Both Ananias and his wife, Sapphira, had agreed together to lie to and to test the Holy Spirit. They didn't have to give anything at all and they certainly were free to give only a portion of their gift had they so chosen.

Their sin was in trying to deceive both the Church and God. As well as telling Ananias that he had lied to God, Peter revealed that Sapphira (just before she also dropped dead) and her husband had agreed together to *test* the Spirit of the Lord.

What did it look and sound like as they took secret counsel together and came up with their plan? One can only imagine. Perhaps they said, "This thing isn't real. We know it looked like that guy at the Beautiful Gate was healed, but maybe they faked it, and all this speaking in tongues and other so-called healings that have been occurring, it's probably mass hysteria or group hypnosis. If it's real, they'll know this isn't the full price, even though we tell them it is."

Their premeditated attempt to test God coupled with their vanity, greed, and lack of trust in God were key components in their hypocrisy. Maybe they wanted the reputation of being known as charter members who had supported the work from the beginning. Perhaps they wanted a reputation like that of Joses (Barnabas) without sacrificing like he had (Acts 4:36–37).

Though we can only imagine their perverse motivation, it was a deliberate, well thought out, and rehearsed act of hypocrisy and deception, and God moved swiftly to judge it.

If they had gotten away with it, lying and double-dealing would have soon spread like leaven through the Church. God dramatically demonstrated (from its inception) how essential integrity is and how destructive deception is to His Church.

We really don't know anything about the background of this couple, but for them to try and perpetrate such an outright falsehood in the middle of such a holy and miraculous atmosphere tells us that they must have been incorrigibly evil. Peter declared that Satan had filled the heart of Ananias. That doesn't happen without willful cooperation.

So we see, in dramatic fashion, God purging His Church. What was the immediate result? "And through the hands of the apostles many signs and wonders were done among the people" (Acts 5:12).

Purity, Prayer, Power, Praise

When Jesus came into the temple, we have a picture of what God wants to see in His Church, for we are the temple of the living God (2 Corinthians 6:16). In Matthew 21, we are told that when Jesus went into the temple He drove out those who were making merchandise of the things of God.

In so doing, He was showing that His temple is to be a place of *purity*. Next He declared that His house was to be a house of *prayer*. Then the blind and lame came to Him in the temple and were healed, showing that His house is to be a house of *power*. Then the children came singing, "Hosanna to the Son of David," showing that His house is to be a house of *praise* (Matthew 21:12–16). *Purity, Prayer, Power,* and *Praise*—may we cooperate fully with the Lord so that all of these attributes can be experienced among His people and in His house.

4. The apostles became His hands and so must we.

Many years ago, at the end of every service at our church, everyone in the church would hold hands as we sang a particular song before we would leave. We called the song "Bringing." The words to that song were:

Bringing, bringing, together we are bringing,
A living Jesus, to a dying world,
Brothers and sisters, together we are bringing,
A living Jesus, to a dying world,
For we're His hands, we're His feet, we're His voice,
And we will speak His name to the nations,
We're His hands, we're His feet, we're His voice,
And we will speak His name to the nations,
Jesus!

As we sang that every week for years, we were both declaring our purpose and reinforcing a truth. The truth is that most of what God does on the earth He does through people. And though He may use any vessel of His choosing at any time for any purpose, we see from the Scriptures that most of what God does on the earth is done through His Church—through yielded people who have given their lives to Him.

In Acts 4:30, when the whole Church lifted their voices in prayer, they asked God to stretch out *His* hands to heal. In Acts 5:12 we are told that "through *the hands of the apostles* many signs and wonders were done among the people" (emphasis mine). They quite literally became the hands of the Lord. God stretched out His hands *through* them.

If I Had as Much Money as You

I remember hearing a story where a missionary came to a local church and shared about the overseas work he was engaged in for the Lord. He also shared how much money they needed to continue their vital work for the next season. A little boy was sitting with his family in that service.

He listened with rapt attention as the missionary told about the exciting opportunities that were before them, and he was amazed as they showed photographs of the tribal people that the missionary was working with.

That evening as the little boy sat at the dinner table with his family, his father, as he did every evening, thanked God for the food, but that night he added something different to his prayer. "And Lord," the father said, "we ask you to meet that missionary's needs and supply everything he needs to carry on. Amen."

When he had finished his prayer, his young son looked up at him and said, "Daddy, if I had as much money as you, I would take care of that missionary's need myself." The father was noticeably shaken. It was as if God had spoken to him at that moment through his son because he did possess ample funds to meet that missionary's need, and when the offering plate had been passed in church that morning, he hadn't put anything in.

We should earnestly pray for God to stretch out His hands to heal, bless, and help, and then, like Isaiah of old, say, "Here I am Lord, send me."

5. The life of the Church consisted of the practical and the spectacular.

> [31] And when they had prayed, the place where they were assembled together was shaken; and they were all filled with the Holy Spirit, and they spoke the word of God with boldness. [32] Now the multitude of those who believed were of one heart and one soul; neither did anyone say that any of the things he possessed was his own, but they had all things in common. [33] And with great power the apostles gave witness to the resurrection of the Lord Jesus. And great grace was upon them all. [34] Nor was there anyone among them who

lacked; for all who were possessors of lands or houses sold them, and brought the proceeds of the things that were sold, ³⁵and laid them at the apostles' feet; and they distributed to each as anyone had need. (Acts 4:31–35)

Doesn't it seem like verse 33 should come after verse 31 instead of what is written in verse 32? The logical thing would be to put verses 31 and 33 together, followed by what is written in verses 32, 34, and 35. But we know that nothing the Holy Spirit inspires (including the order in which things are recorded in Scripture) is random or out of place.

So why is the record of practical needs being met mingled with a record of the Holy Spirit doing supernatural acts?

I believe it can be answered (at least in part) by realizing that the Christian life has the practical and the supernatural intermingled. Though you will always find believers who will notoriously lean more to one side while neglecting the other, a balanced Christian life embraces both.

Thank God for the Marys who always want to sit at Jesus' feet, but without the Marthas we'd never get anything to eat! There is the need of supernatural ministry and the bold preaching of God's Word, but there is also the necessity of meeting practical needs.

6. If we are going to experience the supernatural, we must seek to be constantly filled with the Spirit.

One thing that Dr. Luke made sure was recorded during this explosive season of growth and healing was the fact that Peter and the disciples were filled with the Spirit—*more than once.*

In Acts 2:4, it says of Peter and those in the upper room, "And they were all filled with the Holy Spirit and began to speak with other tongues, as the Spirit gave them utterance."

Acts 4:8 says, "Then Peter, filled with the Holy Spirit, said to them . . ."

And again in Acts 4:31, it is recorded, "And when they had prayed, the place where they were assembled together was shaken; and they were all filled with the Holy Spirit, and they spoke the word of God with boldness."

Filled in Acts 2:4 then again in Acts 4:8 and again in Acts 4:31—one time was not enough.

Peter was filled in the upper room, then at the judgment bar before the Sanhedrin, and then again as they continued to preach. What he had in the upper room wouldn't do for the judgment bar, and what he had at the judgment bar wouldn't suffice for what came next. We need fresh oil for every new challenge and task that we face (Psalm 92:10).

God gives us fresh infillings of His Spirit as needs arise. The Israelites couldn't collect extra manna and store it up. They had to look to God daily to supply them with what they needed, and we must look to God daily to supply us with the measure and anointing of His Spirit for the task or difficulty at hand.

The command to "Be filled with the Spirit," found in Ephesians 5:18, is not a doctrine to be debated but a command to be obeyed. The tense of the verb in Greek speaks of a *continuous action*. It could literally be rendered, "Be continuously in the process of being filled."

If we are going to experience the miraculous things that we read about in the early days of the Church, we cannot overlook the importance of being filled with the Spirit. Those infillings will come as we give ourselves to prayer and as we look to Him in our times of need.

7. No case is too difficult for God.

As we finish this section from the book of Acts, I would like to circle back and talk about something that I hope will encourage you. There has been a flurry of salvations, arrests, preaching, and prayers surrounding the healing of the man at the Beautiful Gate. Every part of the story is rich in lessons to be learned, but let us not forget about God's great love and power that raised that poor man to health.

The Scripture tells us that the man who was healed had been lame from his mother's womb and that he was now more than forty years old (Acts 3:2; 4:22). Can you imagine any case more hopeless? Yet that did not hinder God in the slightest. Nothing is too difficult for our God (Jeremiah 32:17, 27).

Perhaps you have had a lingering illness or are facing a situation that from a human vantage point is unsolvable or beyond aid. That does not limit God. Neither His ability nor His compassion has diminished.

In Psalm 103:2–3, we are told, "Bless the Lord, O my soul, and forget not all His benefits: Who forgives all your iniquities, Who heals all your diseases."

He is the same today and His benefits have not changed. In fact, if anything, they have only increased and become richer because we have a better covenant established upon better promises (Hebrews 8:6).

Look to the Great Physician as your Healer. He loves you so much that He sent His Son to die for you, and if He did that, "how shall He not with Him also freely give you all things" (Romans 8:32)?

CHAPTER
17

Miracles, Martyrs, and More Miracles

As the early church experienced explosive growth, it began to face the kinds of practical challenges that come with multiplying disciples and meeting needs. In Acts 6, we see one of the first internal tensions arise—and how the apostles, led by wisdom and the Spirit, responded with both spiritual focus and practical leadership:

> ¹Now in those days, when the number of the disciples was multiplying, there arose a complaint against the Hebrews by the Hellenists, because their widows were neglected in the daily distribution. ²Then the twelve summoned the multitude of the disciples and said, "It is not desirable that we should leave the word of God and serve tables. ³Therefore, brethren, seek out from among you seven men of good reputation, full of the Holy Spirit and wisdom, whom we may appoint over this business; ⁴but we will give ourselves continually to prayer and to the ministry of the word."

> ⁵And the saying pleased the whole multitude. And they chose Stephen, a man full of faith and the Holy Spirit, and Philip, Prochorus, Nicanor, Timon, Parmenas, and Nicolas, a proselyte from Antioch, ⁶whom they set before the apostles; and when they had prayed, they laid hands on them.
>
> ⁷Then the word of God spread, and the number of the disciples multiplied greatly in Jerusalem, and a great many of the priests were obedient to the faith.
>
> ⁸And Stephen, full of faith and power, did great wonders and signs among the people. (Acts 6:1–8)

As the Church grew, so did the needs. Whether perceived or actual, the Greek-speaking Jews within the burgeoning company of believers felt that their widows were being discriminated against in the daily distribution of food. Up to this point, the Twelve had been responsible for distributing the Church's resources to meet individual needs (Acts 4:34–35), but now the Church was numbering in the thousands and they could no longer keep up.

Realizing that their primary ministry was prayer and the study and teaching of the Word (as it should be with every gospel minister), they had the larger body of believers seek out seven men that were 1) from among them, 2) of good reputation, 3) full of the Holy Spirit, and 4) full of wisdom.

They found seven men (all with Greek names, which was wise because they were not likely to be accused of favoritism by the Greek-speaking, Jewish believers) and brought them before the apostles. The apostles prayed, laid hands on these men, and appointed them over the business of distributing food and serving tables.

The first man on the list was Stephen. We are told that he was filled with two things: *faith* and *power*. Because of this, he did great signs and wonders among the people. The Greek word translated "power" is *dunamis*.

We have already seen that this is a word often used in Scripture to describe God's power to heal physical ailments (Luke 5:17; 6:19; 8:46; 9:1; 10:38). We are also told that through this power Stephen did great wonders and *signs* among the people.

The same word is used in Mark 16:17 where it says that these *signs* will follow those who believe, one of which is laying hands on the sick for their healing (Mark 16:18, 20). This same word is used when describing the healing of the noble man's son, plus many others whom Jesus healed, as well as the miracle of healing that occurred for the lame man at the Beautiful Gate of the temple. In addition to that, it will soon be used to describe numerous healings that would occur in the city of Samaria under the ministry of Philip (John 4:54; 6:2; Acts 4:16, 22; 8:6–7).

A Bow with No Arrow

One reason that it is important to establish that Stephen was being used by God in the arena of healing is because he was *not* an apostle. He was just a member of this growing body of believers called the Church.

God can potentially use anyone, regardless of their title. Yet there were two things that Stephen had that made him a perfect candidate for God to use. He was filled with *faith* and *power*.

Obviously, those two things, though being related, are not the same. In verse 5, we are told that Stephen was full of faith and of the Holy Spirit, and in verse 8 it says that he was full of faith and power. So, being full of the Holy Spirit is synonymous with being full of power.

Faith comes from our intake of the Word and power comes from prayer (Romans 10:17; Acts 4:31).

I have known people who were all about prayer and yet spent little time in the Word of God. I have known others who were all about the Word and yet spent little to no time in prayer. Faith is the catalyst that releases the power. Faith gives direction to power and releases it. Faith without power is like a bow with no arrow, and power without faith is like an arrow with no bow.

Fire and Gunpowder

When I was a kid, a cousin of mine came to spend several weeks with our family one summer. Where we lived, the Fourth of July was always a huge celebration and our city's ordinances allowed individuals and families to light fireworks in the street in front of their homes. My cousin spent that Fourth of July with us.

During the celebrations, the two of us (we were about 12 years old at the time) collected a large arsenal of firecrackers and various fireworks, but we didn't light them. We cut them all open and collected the gunpowder from within them. A couple of days later, we came up with a brilliant idea (or so we thought) concerning what to do with all the gunpowder we had collected.

I had an empty, hard plastic tube that had been used to hold quarters. We packed it full of the gunpowder and screwed the end on tight. Next, we drilled a hole in the side for the fuse. It was going well until we realized we had no way to make the fuse stay in the hole we had drilled.

"I've got it!" my cousin suddenly said. "Wax!" I thought he meant we should find some kind of soft wax and mold it around the fuse, but before I knew it, he had disappeared into the house and come back with a candle and matches.

He lit the candle and began to drip hot wax around the fuse. From about two feet away I watched in amazement—it actually seemed to be working. That is . . . until a piece of the burning wick cascaded down with some of the melting wax.

There was a loud BOOM! My cousin and I were both knocked flat. When I got up my ears were ringing so loud I couldn't hear. My eyebrows were singed as well as the hair hanging down on my forehead. My cousin got the worst of it. He lost most of his eyebrows and quite a bit of his hair was burned off in the front.

Luckily, other than the temporary ringing in our ears, my cousin's sore hand, and the loss of a bit of hair, the damage was minimal. Once that fire and gunpowder got together there was a release of explosive power.

It is that way with the Word of God and prayer. When we get full of faith (from spending unhurried time in the Word) and we get full of the Holy Spirit (from spending undistracted time in prayer), supernatural things will begin happening.

If you read through Acts 7, it becomes obvious why Stephen was so full of faith. It is because he was full of the Word—it came pouring out of him. And I think we can safely assume that he was a man of prayer because he was also full of the Holy Spirit (power).

We don't need to overcomplicate things. If we will give ourselves to the Word and prayer, we will become likely candidates for the Holy Spirit to use us, like Stephen in the arena of healing. We also must embrace the fact that once we do become full of faith and power, we are a more visible target for the enemy. The devil will do all he can to shut down those who are bringing attention to Jesus (as Stephen was).

The Church's First Martyr

The very next thing we read after we are told that Stephen did great wonders and signs among the people is that some arose to dispute with him (Acts 6:8–9). Those who disputed with him found out very quickly that they could not match swords with him verbally, so they quickly resorted to trying to defame him by getting others to falsely accuse him.

After stirring up the crowd, they separated him from the other members of the Church in order to make him vulnerable. He was then brought before the Sanhedrin where more false witnesses accused him of blasphemy (Acts 6:10–15).

Stephen knew full well what they were doing. He could have backed off and compromised, saying, "No, wait, they misunderstood me," but he did no such thing. Instead, he held his ground and boldly told them the truth.

From Acts 7:2–53, he gives a brilliant synopsis of Israel's history, ending by telling them that they were resisting the Holy Spirit and that they were lawbreakers, betrayers, and murderers. It was more truth than they were willing to hear and they killed him for it. Stephen was cast out of the city and stoned to death, even as he called on God to not charge his murderers with the sin of killing him.

He was the Church's first martyr, but he would not be the last. Persecution was going to severely heat up for Christ's Church, but even as it did, the preaching of the gospel and the healing of the sick would continue to spread.

A Few Thoughts About Stephen

Before we move on to Dr. Luke's next recorded section where healings took place, here are a few thoughts about Stephen that are worth considering.

1. Stephen was a disciple, not an apostle.

I realize that this truth has already been stated, but it bears repetition. There are those today who will say, "Yes, God used to heal, but that was only through the apostles." Obviously, that is not true. In fact, in the next section of this book we will explore how God used another of the seven (table waiters) to bring healing to an entire city.

There are others who realize that God still heals today, but in their minds, it has to be through a pastor or some evangelist. They don't think of themselves as being vessels that God might choose to use in the area of healing. My advice is to get full of faith and the Holy Spirit and then begin laying your hands on the sick as Jesus commanded all believers to do (Mark 16:17–18).

2. Stephen did great wonders and signs among the people.

God used him to do the wonders and signs *among the people* whom he was serving by waiting on tables and serving food (Acts 6:8). Look for God to use you where you are right now—at your place of employment and where you serve in your local church.

A Wrong Number . . . or Was It?

Many years ago, one of our secretaries at the church was on her lunch break when she suddenly felt the Holy Spirit urging her to run back into the office area. So she left her lunch and she ran!

As she got back into her office the telephone was ringing. She picked it up and said a breathless "Hello?" It was a wrong number. Someone was calling from Washington, DC, (we were in California), and within about ten seconds they realized they had dialed the wrong number. "I'm sorry," said the secretary, "there's no one here by that name. You have called a church."

"Sorry," the stranger at the other end of the line said, but before they could hang up the secretary said, "Wait! God wants to tell you something." She then proceeded to tell this stranger what God was putting on her heart at that moment.

The person at the other end was stunned (I think they may have even shed a few tears). The "word" that the secretary gave them was exactly what they needed to hear. It spoke so specifically and profoundly into a situation that they were facing, and they knew it was a message from God for them.

That secretary was full of the Holy Spirit and God used her in a significant way—right where she was. There was no pulpit, no microphone, no congregation, just a listening ear and an obedient heart. Let God use you right where you are. Every day we are surrounded by people with needs, people who are hurting and looking for the truth. God is looking for available vessels through which He can pour out His blessings. Will you be one of those vessels?

3. It is a great honor to serve God's people in any capacity.

From reading Stephen's words in Acts 7, it is quite evident that he had a gift for expounding the Word of God. He more than likely also had some sense that God wanted to use him in a miraculous way, yet he had been chosen by the Church, and the apostles had laid hands on him *to serve tables*!

It is worth noting that Stephen didn't say something like, "Hey, wait a minute! Wait on tables? Me? I'm called to teach. I have an anointing for miracles. Don't you have any more discernment than that? I'm not going to lower myself and wait on tables!"

Dear friend, Stephen realized (as we must) that it was, and is, a great honor to serve God's people in any capacity! I think that some never come into what they think of as the greater things because they are unwilling to do what they presently think is lesser, or somehow below them. Jesus said, "Whoever desires to become great among you, let him be your servant" (Matthew 20:26).

4. Stephen was filled with the Spirit for three things.

First, we are told that Stephen was full of the Holy Spirit to *wait on tables* (Acts 6:5). Then we are told that he was full of the Holy Spirit to *work miracles* (Acts 6:8). Finally, we are told that he was full of the Holy Spirit to *be a martyr* for Christ (Acts 7:55).

The third time we are told that he was full of the Spirit is when he died. That is actually a fulfillment of what Jesus said in Acts 1:8, "But you shall receive power when the Holy Spirit has come upon you; and you shall be witnesses to Me in Jerusalem, and in all Judea and Samaria, and to the end of the earth."

The Greek word translated "witnesses" is *martus*. It certainly includes the thought of being a witness for Christ through empowered preaching and through the expression of healing and the miraculous, but we must also remember that *martus* means "martyr." It is what the English word *martyr* is derived from! The idea is that we need the Spirit to fill us in order to live right and to die right!

If our lives are going to truly be a witness for Christ, we must be full of the Spirit, and if our deaths are going to glorify Him and point to Him, we must also be full of the Spirit! When Stephen died, He saw Jesus *standing* at the right hand of God.

Everywhere else in Scripture when it speaks of Jesus at the Father's right hand, He is *sitting*. Why is He standing when Stephen dies? We are not told, but I like to think He was giving Stephen a standing ovation. What a homecoming!

Another of the Seven

After the murder of Stephen, a wave of severe persecution was released upon the church in Jerusalem.

> ¹Now Saul was consenting to his death. At that time a great persecution arose against the church which was at Jerusalem; and they were all scattered throughout the regions of Judea and Samaria, except the apostles. ²And devout men carried Stephen to his burial, and made great lamentation over him. ³As for Saul, he made havoc of the church, entering every house, and dragging off men and women, committing them to prison. ⁴Therefore those who were scattered went everywhere preaching the word. (Acts 8:1–4)

Saul, who had guarded the men's coats while they stoned Stephen to death, didn't just consent to Stephen's death, he did so with pleasure or delight (for so the word depicts in the original Greek).

On the very day of Stephen's burial, a great persecution broke out against the whole church (not just the leaders). As a result, many were scattered, except the apostles, possibly because they still had the sympathy of a great many people and the Jewish leaders were still afraid to harm them, or they were led by God to stay and face the storm.

In verse 3, it says that Saul (later to become the apostle Paul) made *havoc* of the church. That literally means that he treated them with *savage brutality*. Imagine the scene for a moment: believers can no longer be found in public meetings, so Saul begins to forcibly break into the homes of people who are either known to be or suspected to be Christians.

Listen to the apostle Paul's own commentary of this part of his life:

> "I persecuted this Way to the death, binding and delivering into prisons both men and women." (Acts 22:4)

> ⁹"Indeed, I myself thought I must do many things contrary to the name of Jesus of Nazareth. ¹⁰This I also did in Jerusalem, and many of the saints I shut up in prison, having received authority from the chief priests; and when they were put to death, I cast my vote against them. ¹¹And I punished them often in every synagogue and compelled them to blaspheme; and being exceedingly enraged against them, I persecuted them even to foreign cities." (Acts 26:9–11)

Again, the devil's strategy to contain the work of God through persecution backfired. Instead of being subdued, the preaching of the good news only spread. Both Saul and the Jewish leaders had hoped to put out the fire of Christianity by persecution, but they only succeeded in scattering the embers and starting fires in other places.

And one of those embers that had been scattered was Philip, who had been selected to wait on tables beside Stephen. He went down to the city of Samaria armed with the good news that Jesus saves and heals:

> ⁵Then Philip went down to the city of Samaria and preached Christ to them. ⁶And the multitudes with one accord heeded the things spoken by Philip, hearing and seeing the miracles which he did. ⁷For unclean spirits, crying with a loud voice, came out of many who were possessed; and many who were paralyzed and lame were healed. ⁸And there was great joy in that city. (Acts 8:5–8)

The Significance of Going to Samaria

Philip taking the gospel into Samaria is significant for several reasons. First, because it was a fulfillment of the commission that Jesus gave in Acts 1:8, where He said, "But you shall receive power when the Holy Spirit has come upon you; and you shall be witnesses to Me in Jerusalem, and in all Judea and ***Samaria***, and to the end of the earth." But it is also of special interest for several other reasons, especially when you consider the relationship that Israel had with Samaria.

The Jews had no dealings with the Samaritans. They wouldn't fellowship with them under any circumstances because as a whole they viewed them as being inferior. They were descendants of the Northern Kingdom (Samaria being its capital) that remained after the Assyrians conquered them. They intermarried with foreign (non-Jewish) peoples and were considered by pure-blooded Jews to be some sort of half-breeds.

Later, when the Southern Kingdom was conquered by Babylon, its inhabitants refused to lose their Jewish identity. When they returned to Israel to rebuild Jerusalem under Ezra and Nehemiah, they refused to let the Samaritans be involved.

Eventually, the Samaritans built their own temple on Mount Gerizim to rival the temple in Jerusalem. There was an unhealed breach and animosity between these two groups that was centuries old. The gospel was the only solution to the racial and tribal prejudice that existed then, and it is the only solution today. The heart of the problem is the problem of the heart, and Jesus is the only one that can change hearts.

Legislation and political maneuvering, no matter how cleverly enacted or well-intentioned, can't fix what is broken. It takes men and women with burning hearts to change things—burning with the love of God and the truth of the gospel. Such was Philip. He came to Samaria, burning with the news of a living Jesus that could save and heal, and he changed the city.

"It's Only Because of Jesus"

In my lifetime, I have had the privilege to preach the gospel in many nations of the world. One of the places that I have always loved to travel to is Africa. I have ministered in a number of nations on that great continent and I have been blessed to make some lifelong friends from different regions, tribes, and cultures.

In one particular nation where I have preached many times, I learned early on that there was great animosity between two large tribal groups where I was holding meetings. It went far beyond a general suspicion or dislike between them. Things often escalated to fighting and bloodshed.

As I met and spoke with members of each tribe, I could not physically distinguish one group from the other. In fact, the only way I could discern a difference between them was because they spoke different languages. I soon found out that the warfare and hatred between them went back for generations.

One day back home, after preaching on a Sunday morning at our own church, as my habit was, I went out into the lobby to greet and talk with people. While I was there, a couple of African ladies came up to speak to me. They were arm in arm. I didn't think there was anything out of the ordinary about it (as we have many Africans in our church) until they told me what tribes they were from.

They each belonged to different tribes—in fact, they were from the two tribes that historically hated one another. "Pastor, we are best friends!" they told me. "It's only because of Jesus!" Jesus changes hearts! Now Philip goes into despised Samaria and preaches Christ to them. What an impact he had!

Healing Miracles Were Tied to the Preaching of Christ

Philip's message to the Samaritans was *Christ*. That should be our message to the unsaved as well. And as we saw in Philip's ministry, I believe that we should expect to see healing miracles tied to the preaching of Christ today. God confirms His Word with accompanying signs (Mark 16:17, 20).

If we boldly preach the message of a risen, compassionate Savior who is the same yesterday, today, and forever, we should expect to see miracles accompanying our preaching as well (Hebrews 13:8).

In Samaria, hearing of and seeing the healings that were occurring, as well as observing people being set free from evil spirits, only served to cause people to more intently heed the message of salvation that Philip preached.

These supernatural, Holy Spirit-wrought signs were of particular consequence, for as we shall see, the people of Samaria had already witnessed the false supernatural.

> [9]But there was a certain man called Simon, who previously practiced sorcery in the city and astonished the people of Samaria, claiming that he was someone great, [10]to whom they all gave heed, from the least to the greatest, saying, "This man is the great power of God." [11]And they heeded him because he had astonished them with his sorceries for a long time. [12]But when they believed Philip as he preached the things concerning the kingdom of God and the name of Jesus Christ, both men and women were baptized. [13]Then Simon himself also believed; and when he was baptized he continued with Philip, and was amazed, seeing the miracles and signs which were done. (Acts 8:9–13)

There is a false supernatural, or a supernatural that finds its origin in the devil. When Moses and Aaron performed (at the direction of God) their miraculous signs before Pharaoh in Egypt, Pharaoh's magicians were able to imitate some of those same miraculous signs (to a lesser degree). Speaking of the coming of the antichrist, Paul said that it will be "according to the working of Satan, with all power, signs and lying wonders" (2 Thessalonians 2:9).

Before the coming of Philip, there had been an agent of the devil in Samaria named Simon who had astonished the people of Samaria with his sorceries. But as with Moses and Aaron and the magicians of Egypt, the miracles that were done through Philip far outstripped anything that Simon had previously done, to the point that Simon himself was amazed when he saw what was happening.

When Simon did his sorcery and signs, he claimed to be great himself. When Philip did his signs and miracles, he claimed that Jesus was great! The true supernatural always leads men to Christ. He is the focal point, not the vessel He is using.

A Few More Observations and Thoughts

Before we move on to the next account of miraculous healing given by Dr. Luke in the book of Acts, I would like to share some final thoughts and observations about Philip and how God used him in Samaria.

1. Like Stephen, Philip was not an apostle.

He was one of the seven men chosen to help serve food to members of the Jerusalem church. He later became known as Philip the Evangelist, but that was later in his ministry (Acts 21:8).

When Philip did not have a title (except being *one of the seven*), he was used mightily by God in the arenas of soul winning and healing. I believe that was mostly because he went and did something. He obeyed the commission that Jesus gave to His Church, and as he did, the Holy Spirit showed up in power. If we want to see miraculous results like Philip, we need to first step out in simple obedience and do something like Philip did.

2. God can use one person to impact many.

Philip was one man, yet he influenced multitudes. An entire city was set ablaze for Christ because of one man's willingness to go and bring the good news to people in need (Acts 8:6–8). May we never make the mistake of underestimating what God can do through our simple acts of obedience.

3. It seems that Philip had success in bringing healing to only certain kinds of maladies.

It is interesting to note that in addition to casting out demons, something every believer has been commissioned to do (Mark 16:17), Philip had great success in bringing healing to those who were paralyzed or lame.

No mention is made of the blind receiving their sight or of deaf ears being opened. Why is that? Perhaps those things did occur and the scriptural record just didn't mention it, but it may be due to something else that is worth considering.

In 1 Corinthians 12, the apostle Paul teaches about the different gifts or manifestations of the Spirit that are given to individual members of the Church. First Corinthians 12:4–11 declares,

> [4]There are diversities of gifts, but the same Spirit. [5]There are differences of ministries, but the same Lord. [6]And there are diversities of activities, but it is the same God who works all in all. [7]But the manifestation of the Spirit is given to each

one for the profit of all: ⁸for to one is given the word of wisdom through the Spirit, to another the word of knowledge through the same Spirit, ⁹to another faith by the same Spirit, to another gifts of healings by the same Spirit, ¹⁰to another the working of miracles, to another prophecy, to another discerning of spirits, to another different kinds of tongues, to another the interpretation of tongues. ¹¹But one and the same Spirit works all these things, distributing to each one individually as He wills.

There are nine different gifts or manifestations listed, one being the *gifts of healings*. It is interesting to note that this particular gift is stated in the plural. In fact, both the words *gifts* and *healings* are in plural form in the Greek (hence it is translated that way in English).

The idea is that there is actually a series of gifts within this gift (imagine a bunch of grapes on one stem) and that certain aspects of this gift work to heal specific maladies. It may be that when someone is endowed with such a gift, like Philip, it wouldn't be all the gifts of healings but only a part.

So it may well be that Philip had the gifts of healings that worked to heal paralysis and similar maladies, but not for all types of sickness. In fact, it has been my experience that those ministers whom God particularly uses in the arena of healing in our day seem to have far greater success with certain types of diseases than with others.

Jesus would have been endowed with the full measure or expression of this gift because He had the Spirit without measure (John 3:34). Therefore, He healed all manner of sickness and disease, but no single member of the Church would have the Spirit without measure like Jesus did. We are dependent upon one another. No one person has it all or can do it all. We are an interconnected body with Jesus as our head (1 Corinthians 12:12–26; Colossians 1:18).

I simply submit my thoughts along these lines for your consideration. It is one possible explanation for the absence (by mention) of other sicknesses being healed under the ministry of Philip at Samaria, but it is not the only possible explanation.

It is also worth mentioning that just because a minister or individual may have a limited expression of the gifts of healings in their life or ministry, that does not stop a believer from praying the prayer of faith to receive healing from any malady. Nor would it somehow cancel out the results that can be wrought through believers, as they, in simple obedience to the command of Jesus, lay hands on the sick.

No One Has It All or Can Do It All

Along these same lines, it is pretty obvious if you read through the whole account of Philip's ministry in Samaria that he was not equipped to do everything.

> [14] Now when the apostles who were at Jerusalem heard that Samaria had received the word of God, they sent Peter and John to them, [15] who, when they had come down, prayed for them that they might receive the Holy Spirit. [16] For as yet He had fallen upon none of them. They had only been baptized in the name of the Lord Jesus. [17] Then they laid hands on them, and they received the Holy Spirit. [18] And when Simon saw that through the laying on of the apostles' hands the Holy Spirit was given, he offered them money, [19] saying, "Give me this power also, that anyone on whom I lay hands may receive the Holy Spirit." [20] But Peter said to him, "Your money perish with you, because you thought that the gift of God could be purchased with money! [21] You

have neither part nor portion in this matter, for your heart is not right in the sight of God. ²²Repent therefore of this your wickedness, and pray God if perhaps the thought of your heart may be forgiven you. ²³For I see that you are poisoned by bitterness and bound by iniquity." ²⁴Then Simon answered and said, "Pray to the Lord for me, that none of the things which you have spoken may come upon me." ²⁵So when they had testified and preached the word of the Lord, they returned to Jerusalem, preaching the gospel in many villages of the Samaritans. (Acts 8:14–25)

Here are a few more thoughts regarding our need for one another, gleaned from the account of Philip in Samaria:

1. Philip had one message. That was Christ. The only other time we find him preaching is to the Ethiopian eunuch and his message to him was Jesus (Acts 8:5, 35). Apparently, he wasn't gifted to teach the Word like Stephen had been, so before leaving Samaria, Peter and John did preach the Word to these new believers to help them get grounded in their faith (v. 25).

2. Apparently Philip was not anointed to get people filled with the Holy Spirit. Peter and John came and did that as well (vv. 15–17).

3. Obviously Philip was not very discerning. The Scripture declared that once Simon was baptized he continued with Philip (Acts 8:13). One translation says that he attached himself to Philip. The actual Greek word carries with it the thought of "attending as a student" or as a protégé. Simon was not the best candidate that Philip could have found, for Simon's heart was not right and he was poisoned by bitterness and bound by iniquity. Peter

discerned Simon's wicked motives while Philip didn't seem to see them at all (vv. 18–25). (The word simony, which means "the buying or selling of ecclesiastical privileges, favors, or positions," is derived from this story.)

Everyone I Appoint Splits the Church

I had a dear friend who pastored a growing, vibrant church. He was a good preacher and he genuinely loved the people of his flock, but by his own admission, he was not very gifted when it came to spiritual discernment. He told me one day, "Everyone that I appoint to a position of authority splits the church and tries to take over. I have no discernment when it comes to people."

And I had watched it happen. Their growth and momentum were stifled again and again by church splits caused by people whom he had appointed who were greedy for power. Is the answer to a situation like that to quit? No. Obviously not. I believe the answer is twofold.

First, pray to be more discerning, and second, rely on trusted people who are more discerning than you are. In my friend's case, he needed to start listening to his wife. She had warned him several times in the past not to appoint certain people, but he wouldn't listen. He paid a steep price for not relying on her discernment, but he eventually learned his lesson.

We need every member of the body of Christ. Philip needed Peter and John, Peter and John needed Philip. No one has it all or can do it all. The sooner we realize and embrace that truth, the better off we will be.

CHAPTER
18

Aeneas and Dorcas

As we follow Philip's story, we find him (first at the direction of an angel and then directly by the Holy Spirit) going out into the desert where he meets an Ethiopian man of great authority who was sitting in his chariot. Philip leads him to Christ and then baptizes him.

The Spirit then "catches Philip away," and we find him next at Azotus. From there he preached in all the coastal cities until he came to Caesarea, where he apparently began to reside. If you look on a map at the route that Philip would have taken, it is significant because as we look at the next biblical record of divine healing, it takes place through the ministry of Peter . . . in the very places where Philip would have traveled and preached.

He Entered into Philip's Labors

> [32] Now it came to pass, as Peter went through all parts of the country, that he also came down to the saints who dwelt in

Lydda. ³³There he found a certain man named Aeneas, who had been bedridden eight years and was paralyzed. ³⁴And Peter said to him, "Aeneas, Jesus the Christ heals you. Arise and make your bed." Then he arose immediately. ³⁵So all who dwelt at Lydda and Sharon saw him and turned to the Lord. (Acts 9:32–35)

As Peter was traveling through all parts of the country (apparently to strengthen the believers everywhere the Church had been established and souls had been won), he came to Lydda where there was a group of believers.

More than likely, these converts were the fruit of Philip's ministry. In a very real sense, Peter is entering into (again) Philip's labors. In Lydda there was a man who was paralyzed and bedridden for eight years (a detail that Luke, in his typical thorough fashion as a physician, records).

The words that Peter spoke to Aeneas were almost identical to the command that Jesus gave to the sick man lying on his bed by the pool of Bethesda: "Rise, take up your bed and walk" (John 5:8). Truly, as Luke told Theophilus in his opening words to the book of Acts, the Gospel that he had formerly written (the Gospel according to Luke) was a record of what Jesus *began* to do and teach (Acts 1:1).

He began, but He wasn't finished. He is still healing years after His resurrection, but now He is using members of His Church to carry on those works. Peter made that clear when he said, "Aeneas, Jesus the Christ heals you."

Healed of Stomach Cancer

Many years ago, a husband and wife came to our church out of desperation. They were not Christians, but they heard that people at our church prayed for the sick and that genuine healing had taken place.

The wife had been taking treatments for stomach cancer but was progressively getting worse.

We met with them and shared from the Scriptures how Jesus is the same today as He was when He walked the shores of Galilee. We had them read certain promises from the Bible on healing and on prayer. We then laid hands on her and prayed for her healing.

A few days later, they returned to the church absolutely ecstatic. When she went back to the doctor, no trace of the cancer could be found. After a series of X-rays, her puzzled doctor said, "It looks like your cancer has disappeared!"

The first thing that the couple did was give their hearts to Jesus. All of their children followed suit. The next week, they were all sitting together in church. The wife and husband began volunteering and over the next several decades they became permanent fixtures in the church, faithfully following the Lord and serving His people.

As we read the story of Aeneas, we find that his healing (like the woman in our church) served as a catalyst to bring many to the Lord. The Scripture tells us that "all who dwelt at Lydda and Sharon saw him and turned to the Lord" (Sharon refers to an entire coastal region between Joppa and Mount Carmel).

The same thing happened when the lame man was healed at the Beautiful Gate in Jerusalem. It happened when people were healed under the ministry of Philip in Samaria, and now we see it happening in Lydda and Sharon. God has not changed. Healing is part of His plan to help turn people's eyes heavenward and to help their hearts become receptive to the gospel message.

Next Stop, Joppa

> ³⁶At Joppa there was a certain disciple named Tabitha, which is translated Dorcas. This woman was full of good works and charitable deeds which she did. ³⁷But it happened in those days that she became sick and died. When they had washed her, they laid her in an upper room. ³⁸And since Lydda was near Joppa, and the disciples had heard that Peter was there, they sent two men to him, imploring him not to delay in coming to them. ³⁹Then Peter arose and went with them. When he had come, they brought him to the upper room. And all the widows stood by him weeping, showing the tunics and garments which Dorcas had made while she was with them. (Acts 9:36–39)

Tabitha is Hebrew and Dorcas is Greek for "gazelle." This gazelle was a disciple of Jesus. She was *full* of good works and charitable deeds. She didn't just *talk* about helping others (as many do). She didn't just *intend* to do good works (as many plan yet never follow through on).

These were good works and charitable deeds, *which she did*. She had even personally made coats and garments to clothe widows! This woman had put the gospel in work clothes and let her light shine before men (Matthew 5:16). Yet, despite the fact that she was a follower of Christ and that her life was full of good works, she became sick and died.

Bad Things Sometimes Happen to Good People

This tells us several things. First, *bad things sometimes happen to good people*. We are living in a fallen world and everything does not operate the way that God originally intended it to. We also have an enemy running loose whose sole agenda is to kill, steal, and destroy.

Eventually, the devil will be forever removed from human contact (when he's thrown into the lake of fire), and God will ultimately create a new heaven and a new earth (John 10:10; 1 Peter 5:8–9; Revelation 20:10; 2 Peter 3:10–13; Revelation 21:1). In the meantime, we are here as sojourners and pilgrims whose aim it is to please God as we walk by faith and not by sight (1 Peter 2:11; 2 Corinthians 5:7; Hebrews 11:6).

The second thing that stands out about this story is that *good works are not a shield against the enemy's attacks*. Many times I have been asked, "Why did so and so get sick, or die? They loved God, were generous, and lived an exemplary Christian life. Why?" To which I answer, "I don't know."

But I do know that if people try to use their good works (however numerous or noble) as grounds to persuade God to heal them, it will never happen. Like the forgiveness of sins, healing is a gift of God's grace. It is not earned, it is to be accepted by faith. Faith is the hand that reaches out and accepts what the hand of God's grace freely provides.

Whether it is a promise of forgiveness, guidance, restoration, or healing, that promise will remain unfulfilled until it is accepted by faith. The promises of God are like seeds that are full of potential, yet will lay dormant until they are touched by faith. I can have a perfectly healthy seed that will grow into a healthy, fruitful tree, but if that seed remains in a tray on my nightstand and is never planted, the potential within it will never be released.

The Israelites of old had been promised by God that they would inherit and dwell in the Promised Land, yet the generation that the promise was given to never saw its fulfillment. Hebrews tells us why: "We received the same promises as those people in the wilderness, but the promises didn't do them a bit of good because they didn't receive the promises with faith" (Hebrews 4:2 MSG).

He Was Drunk and Had Abandoned His Family

When I was a new Christian I was attending a small gospel meeting near the town of Klamath Falls, Oregon. My friends and I had arrived early. While they went inside the tiny building, I remained outside to pray. A few days before this, I had gotten a serious infection in one of my eyes and it was completely swollen shut. I was praying for the success of the meeting and I was also trusting God for my eye to become normal again.

Just before the meeting was to begin, I noticed a man who was slowly moving my way. He was dragging one of his legs as he shuffled along. It was obvious to see that he was partially paralyzed. When I walked over to speak to him, something else became very obvious. He was drunk . . . really drunk.

I engaged him in conversation only to find out that he had left his wife and child that very night. He was abandoning them. In fact, he was headed out of town, never to come back. I told him that he should come in to the meeting, which he immediately declined.

I persisted, and eventually he agreed to come in for a few minutes. When we got inside, someone ushered him up and sat him in the front row while I quietly took a seat in the back.

The evangelist that night was what you'd call "a preaching machine." He walked back and forth. He waved his arms like he was fighting bees. He shouted and he preached the Word. He preached that Jesus was a healer and he enthusiastically shared some of the promises about healing.

Right in the middle of his sermon, he turned to the drunk man I had brought in and said, "**Stand up. Jesus is healing you!**" Without hesitation, that man jumped up and began running back and forth—

completely made whole. He started to shout and cry, and so did many of the other people in that meeting. The man then, on the spot, gave his heart to Jesus.

Then the evangelist asked him, "How did you get here tonight?" "A guy brought me in," he said, and then he started looking around. When he spotted me he said, "There he is, in the back." Everyone turned around to see the *messenger* who had brought him into the meeting. And there I was, one eye swollen completely shut, sitting in the back row. I wanted to disappear!

I have thought back on that night many times throughout the years. It was obvious that the man who was miraculously healed and then saved had not merited anything from God. He was drunk and he had just abandoned his wife and child. He simply embraced a promise with simple faith.

It is also obvious that my good works didn't somehow merit or convince God to heal me. Eventually my eye became normal, but it was a process. What a contrast it was! The guy who had driven almost two hours to attend the meeting, who was outside praying, who convinced the drunk to come into the building was still suffering with a painful eye problem. Yet the guy who had gotten drunk, left his family, wasn't even thinking about God, and had ended up in the meeting without a plan or purpose was dramatically healed!

The Secret Things

Had Dorcas or those around her embraced the promises in simple faith? We don't know. Inspired by the Holy Spirit, King David said,

> [1]Those who help the poor succeed will get many blessings. When trouble comes, the Lord will save them. [2]The Lord will protect them and save their lives. He will bless

them in this land. He will not let their enemies harm them.
³When they are sick in bed, the Lord will give them strength
and make them well! (Psalm 41:1–3 ERV)

Dorcas had fulfilled all of the conditions to this promise, yet she did not get well. She died. Were the promises in these verses like those unplanted seeds whose potential was never released? Was the case of Dorcas like the Israelites, who didn't receive the promises with faith?

Again, we are not told, so we don't know. It is one possible explanation, but God in His wisdom did not give us any details as to exactly why she died. So, even though it may have been the reason, since we are not told, it only becomes guesswork and speculation on our part.

"Why even share that?" you might well ask. Because the fact is that none of us has all the answers. There will always be some things we will not understand. Things that God has not given us clear answers to. We must be content to live with that. God is wiser than we are and He lets us know what we need to know. Some answers will have to wait until we get to heaven. The secret things still belong to the Lord (Deuteronomy 29:29).

He Took His Cue from Jesus

> ⁴⁰But Peter put them all out, and knelt down and prayed. And turning to the body he said, "Tabitha, arise." And she opened her eyes, and when she saw Peter she sat up. ⁴¹Then he gave her his hand and lifted her up; and when he had called the saints and widows, he presented her alive. ⁴²And it became known throughout all Joppa, and many believed on the Lord. (Acts 9:40–42)

When Jesus came to the home of Jairus, he was met (like Peter when he was brought to the upper room where the body of Dorcas lay) by a large group of people weeping and mourning over the daughter of Jairus, who had just died. Before raising the little girl from the dead, Jesus put all the mourners outside (Luke 8:51–54).

Peter took his cue from Jesus and did the same thing. It may be that they were affecting the atmosphere in a negative way (after all, the mourners had ridiculed Jesus—they certainly weren't joining Him in faith). When Jesus came to His hometown, *He could not* do any miracles there because of the community's unbelief (Mark 6:1–6), which tells us that unbelief, especially when it is held in common by a group of people, can hinder what God wants to do in their midst.

Psalm 78:41 tells us that due to their unbelief (and their short memory of how God had helped them in the past), the people *limited* the Holy One of Israel.

He Knelt Down and Prayed

The situation with Dorcas would require far more than just praying for a sick person to recover. She had died. Her spirit had left her body. During His earthly ministry, Jesus Himself (as far as we are told in the Gospels) only raised three people from the dead. Peter knew that it would take an extraordinary miracle to call her spirit back and then bring her corpse back to life.

What was God leading Peter to do? He had been summoned by two messengers from Lydda (apparently in hopes that Dorcas could be raised to life), but was raising this woman part of God's plan or was it just the hope of some people who loved her? Was Peter there to attend a funeral or prevent one?

When you don't know what to do, pray! Peter knelt down, and as he did, he faced away from the body. Perhaps he did that so his faith wouldn't be shaken. He had learned his lesson about what can happen when you put your attention on the wind and the waves instead of on Jesus (Matthew 14:29–31).

When Hezekiah of old was told by Isaiah that he would die, he turned his face to the wall and prayed. By turning his face to the wall, he was, in essence, turning away from human opinions and human answers and looking to God alone. And he got his answer. God added fifteen years to his life (2 Kings 20:1–6). There are times when we must "turn away" when we pray, shutting out every voice but God's.

When Peter had received his answer, he turned to the body and said "arise" (the same thing that Jesus had said to the daughter of Jairus). And like the little girl of Jairus, Dorcas opened her eyes and sat up. Then Peter presented her alive to all the saints and widows. What a celebration must have ensued! News of this miracle swiftly spread throughout Joppa, and as it was with the healing of Aeneas in Lydda, many in Joppa believed in the Lord.

We Don't Know Their Names

Two unnamed disciples came from Joppa to Lydda and implored Peter to come with them to Joppa. Who were they? What are their stories? We don't know, but one thing is sure, *we wouldn't have the miracle of Dorcas being raised from the dead and all the subsequent salvations in Joppa without them*!

So much vital kingdom work is carried out by people who will never be known or applauded in this life, but they certainly will be rewarded in heaven. The spiritual domino effect of miracles and salvations (sometimes that can be traced generationally) that result from a simple invitation to attend a church service can be staggering.

Never underestimate what God might do through your simple act of obedience. It may be sharing your testimony with someone at work, inviting a friend or neighbor to come with you to church, or getting out of your bed and on to your knees when you have a burden to pray. I am convinced that when the rewards will be passed out in heaven, there will be lots of surprises.

There are those on earth now who are faithfully following and obeying the Lord and His Word (even in seemingly small ways) and remain unknown to us, but in heaven they are held in reverence and esteem by companies of angels. Endeavor always to have a heart that is sensitive to the Holy Spirit's directions and a will that is prompt to obey. You never know what great things God might accomplish through what you do.

CHAPTER

19

Sent Out by the Holy Spirit

In Acts 13, we find the account of how Paul and Barnabas were sent out by the Holy Spirit on their first missionary journey from their home church in Antioch of Syria. They had great success in winning people to Christ, but they also experienced great persecution.

When they preached in Antioch of Pisidia, many Jews, Jewish proselytes, and Gentiles became Christ followers, but certain envious Jews publicly opposed them and raised up persecution to the point where Paul and Barnabas were physically expelled from the region. Paul and Barnabas shook the dust from their feet (as Jesus had instructed His disciples to do) and they moved on to the city of Iconium, some fifty miles distant (Acts 13:1–52; Luke 9:5).

> ¹Now it happened in Iconium that they went together to the synagogue of the Jews, and so spoke that a great multitude both of the Jews and of the Greeks believed. ²But the unbelieving Jews stirred up the Gentiles and poisoned their

minds against the brethren. ³Therefore they stayed there a long time, speaking boldly in the Lord, who was bearing witness to the word of His grace, granting signs and wonders to be done by their hands. (Acts 14:1–3)

Things in Iconium played out in a similar fashion. They preached Christ in the local synagogue and a great multitude of both Jews and Greeks believed, but the unbelieving Jews (no doubt fueled by jealousy as those in Antioch of Pisidia had been) stirred up persecution against the apostles. Yet in this case, rather than leaving because of the opposition, they stayed there a long time, boldly declaring the gospel. They did not continue to labor there because of the success of their work, but because of the difficulties.

The main differences we find between the situation in Antioch of Pisidia and Iconium were twofold: first, the persecution reached the level of Christians being physically cast out of the region by those in Antioch whereas the persecution in Iconium was mainly verbal, as the unbelieving Jews sought to poison people's minds against the truth. And secondly, at Iconium, the Lord granted that signs and wonders be done through the hands of Paul and Barnabas.

The Word of His Grace

Paul and Barnabas stayed a long time in Iconium speaking boldly in the Lord. What were they proclaiming? "The word of His grace" (v. 3). They weren't preaching salvation by works. They were preaching a message of undeserved favor. That is what the Lord was bearing witness to by granting signs and wonders to be done.

Forgiveness is a gift that is freely given by God. It is by grace through faith, not of works (Ephesians 2:8–9). Healing is no different. It was purchased by Christ through His suffering and cannot be earned or merited through personal sacrifice, generosity, or pious living. It is a free gift that is offered by grace and must be received by faith.

Let's say that I want to give you a brand-new car. I paid for it with money that I earned through my own labor. I don't want anything in exchange for it. It is a gift, pure and simple. But you feel like you need to do something to pay me. "No," I say, as I extend my hand trying to give you the keys. "It is a gift, you can't pay for it."

"But I feel like I need to give you something for it," you say, "It is such a nice car. How about a thousand dollars?"

"No," I respond. "You can't pay for it. If you did, it would no longer be a gift."

"Well, how about five hundred dollars?" you respond. "At least let me give you that. I know that you paid a lot for the car." "No."

"How about two hundred and fifty dollars?" "No." "A hundred dollars?" "No." "Fifty dollars?" "No." "Twenty dollars?" "No! If you even try and give me one dollar, the car is no longer a gift."

It is the same with salvation and all aspects thereof. Whether it is forgiveness or healing or the baptism in the Holy Spirit, it is not earned, period. It comes by grace through faith plus zero.

The signs and wonders that were being done, which confirmed the word of His grace, no doubt included healing, for those same designations are used in connection with healing elsewhere in the New Testament (Mark 16:17–18; John 4:46–54; 6:2; Acts 4:30).

And it says that the signs and wonders were being "done by their hands" (v. 3). When you consider how many times Jesus laid His hands upon the sick to heal them along with the Lord's command for believers to lay hands on the sick for healing, it would be hard to imagine these signs and wonders not including the supernatural healing of the sick (Mark 6:5; 8:23–25; 16:18; Luke 4:40; 13:13; Acts 5:12; 28:8).

Things Heated Up

The persecution began as the unbelieving Jews began to poison people's minds against Paul and Barnabas and the gospel they preached, but after a time, things began to escalate, causing the apostles to move on to other cities.

> [4]But the multitude of the city was divided: part sided with the Jews, and part with the apostles. [5]And when a violent attempt was made by both the Gentiles and Jews, with their rulers, to abuse and stone them, [6]they became aware of it and fled to Lystra and Derbe, cities of Lycaonia, and to the surrounding region. [7]And they were preaching the gospel there. (Acts 14:4–7)

It seems that a great division occurred wherever Paul and Barnabas preached the gospel, even as Christ predicted. He said, "Do not think that I came to bring peace on earth. I did not come to bring peace but a sword" (Matthew 10:34). And like a sword, the gospel message penetrates hearts, but it also brings a separation. There is no middle ground when it comes to Christ. If you are not for Him, you are against Him. If you are not gathering, you are scattering (Luke 11:23).

A Notable Miracle in Lystra

> [8]And in Lystra a certain man without strength in his feet was sitting, a cripple from his mother's womb, who had never walked. [9]This man heard Paul speaking. Paul, observing him intently and seeing that he had faith to be healed, [10]said with a loud voice, "Stand up straight on your feet!" And he leaped and walked. (Acts 14:8–10)

Again we see Luke the physician's eye for medical details. He not only notes that the crippled man was utterly unable to walk (the literal meaning of "without strength in his feet"), but he also tells us that the duration of the man's condition had been since birth.

We are not told where Paul was preaching in Lystra or where exactly the crippled man was sitting who was listening to Paul, but it very well may have been on the street, for there was no synagogue in Lystra. It was a Roman garrison town and a center for Roman culture. Its citizens were mainly pagan.[1]

Imagine the scene. Paul has the attention of a crowd as he boldly preaches the gospel. They are not from a Jewish background, so he is not referencing all the Hebrew prophecies as he normally does when preaching in a synagogue. He is just declaring the truth of a God who so loved the world that He sent His Son to die for their sins. He is preaching about a resurrected Savior who has all power, who is the same yesterday, today, and forever, who is ready to save all who come to Him in faith.

As Paul looks out over the listening crowd, his attention is drawn to a poor cripple. As Paul intently beholds him, he suddenly perceives that the man has faith to be healed. That brings us to an intriguing thought . . . that through the insight given by the Holy Spirit, faith in another can be perceived. Generally, we know someone has faith by observing their actions, for faith is expressed through action (James 2:18). But before there is action, there is the dawning of faith in the heart, and that can only be perceived in someone else by a revelation from the Holy Spirit.

Receive the Holy Spirit!

Many years ago I was preaching on a Sunday morning on the baptism of the Holy Spirit and speaking in tongues. As I was preaching, my attention was drawn to a woman sitting in the congregation. I can't tell you exactly how I knew, but suddenly, I was aware that she had faith to be filled.

I stopped preaching and pointed to her, telling her to stand. I then said in a loud voice, "Receive the Holy Spirit!" She immediately began to speak in other tongues. I don't believe that I ever finished my message that morning, for people began to rejoice and join that woman in worship and prayer. It was a service I never shall forget.

Where Did He Get the Faith to Be Healed?

Where did the cripple at Lystra get the faith to be healed? He got it the same place that the woman that morning got the faith to be filled with the Spirit—from hearing the Word preached. Faith comes by hearing and hearing by the Word of God (Romans 10:17).

Paul was preaching the gospel at Lystra and the man was listening (Acts 14:7–9). The gospel is basically the message that Jesus saves, He heals, He baptizes in the Holy Spirit, and He is coming again. Paul was certainly not preaching that God no longer heals today. There is no way that the man could have derived faith to be healed from a message like that!

With so much preaching today that tells people the days of miracles have passed and that God no longer heals, I am surprised that we see as many people healed as we do. In fact, many people have to unlearn some wrong things they have been taught before they can embrace the right things that belong to the unchanging gospel of Jesus Christ.

It is a noteworthy fact that this miracle of healing at Lystra occurred eighteen years after the birth of the Church on the day of Pentecost (recorded in Acts 2). God was healing then and He is still healing today.

Out of the Frying Pan

As we continue reading the account of what happened at Lystra, we could say that Paul and Barnabas got out of the frying pan and into the fire.

As noted earlier, Lystra was a Roman garrison town. There was not a synagogue there or much Jewish influence. The majority of its citizens would have been believers in a myriad of Greek and Roman gods. When the people saw the miracle that had been performed on the crippled man, they immediately began to think that Paul and Barnabas were Greek deities that had appeared to them in the flesh.

> [11]Now when the people saw what Paul had done, they raised their voices, saying in the Lycaonian language, "The gods have come down to us in the likeness of men!" [12]And Barnabas they called Zeus, and Paul, Hermes, because he was the chief speaker. [13]Then the priest of Zeus, whose temple was in front of their city, brought oxen and garlands to the gates, intending to sacrifice with the multitudes. (Acts 14:11–13)

Apparently, neither Paul nor Barnabas initially understood what the crowd was doing. That was probably because the people were speaking in the local dialect of the Lycaonians. The apostles wouldn't have known what they were saying, but it soon became clear what they were intending to do. Paul and Barnabas were endeavoring to turn the people's hearts to worship the one true God, but now the people were about to begin worshiping them!

> [14]But when the apostles Barnabas and Paul heard this, they tore their clothes and ran in among the multitude, crying out [15]and saying, "Men, why are you doing these things? We also are men with the same nature as you, and preach

to you that you should turn from these useless things to the living God, who made the heaven, the earth, the sea, and all things that are in them, [16]who in bygone generations allowed all nations to walk in their own ways. [17]Nevertheless He did not leave Himself without witness, in that He did good, gave us rain from heaven and fruitful seasons, filling our hearts with food and gladness." [18]And with these sayings they could scarcely restrain the multitudes from sacrificing to them. (Acts 14:14–18)

Persecution to Praise

The opposition the apostles previously faced was verbal persecution, defamation, and abuse, but now they are facing something far more dangerous. The people want to praise and worship them. There is something in our human nature that compels us to worship, but for many people that worship is misplaced. People commonly pour adulations on sports figures or upon famous musicians, singers, or actors, and sometimes, even on preachers. The reality is, however, that only one being is worthy of our worship and that is our Creator.

The Lycaonians were in the process of celebrating and about to offer sacrifices to Paul and Barnabas. What a change it must have been for them. They are used to being maligned and run out of town, not adored. There is something seductive about the praise and adoration of others. The desire for it is what made Lucifer into the devil, and he knows that it is an effective snare for some people.

Now I Am Your Disciple

Many years ago a local paper did a human interest article on my story. The title of the article was "From Drug User to Soul Saver." In the article they shared the story of how I met Christ and was delivered from drugs. They followed up with how my wife and I began our church in a small storefront.

About a week after the article came out I got a call from someone at the paper asking me if I wouldn't mind giving a certain gentleman a call. It seems that he had been repeatedly calling the paper after reading the article.

He kept telling them that he needed to find God. "We can't help you with that," they told him, "but maybe the man we wrote the article about can." They gave me his number and I called him. When I spoke with him, the first thing I noticed was that he had a strong Indian accent. He had been born in India and had immigrated to the US many years before.

I agreed to meet with him the following day. When he came into my office, I was immediately taken with his stature and bearing. He was a tall man with a full head of silver hair. He was immaculately dressed in a suit and tie. After introductions he sat across from me and related how he had been searching for God and that the article in the paper had arrested his attention. "I want to know the God," he said in his thick accent.

I shared the gospel story with him and what the New Testament said about putting your trust in Jesus alone for salvation. After I had shared, we bowed our heads and I led him in a salvation prayer. He confessed Jesus as his Lord and Savior.

When we finished, he smiled and looked at me and said, "Now I am your disciple!"

"I will help you all I can," I told him. "And I want you to start coming to church, but you are a disciple of Jesus, not my disciple. We are both following Him."

The New Testament tells us that men will arise in the Church "to draw away disciples after themselves." It is something that leaders or anyone used by God needs to guard against (Acts 20:28–31).

Our hearts, apart from the influence of the Holy Spirit, can be easily tempted by pride, and that, in the end, will lead to destruction. We need to stay little in our own eyes and always keep the focus on Jesus. If someone pays us a compliment, we should graciously say thank you but at the end of the day get on our knees and lift those compliments to the Lord to whom they truly belong (Proverbs 16:18; 1 Samuel 15:17).

Cheers and Jeers

When I was a young preacher, I had a seasoned minister give me some valuable advice. He said, "Son, don't listen to the cheers or the jeers. If you do (pay attention to them), it can potentially derail you." I have never forgotten that.

If the devil cannot get you to quit because of trouble and outward pressure, he will try and get you to fall through the inward lure of pride. And it is amazing how fickle people can be. The ones who want to crown you one minute may try and crucify you the next.

The very next verse in Acts 14 says,

> Then Jews from Antioch and Iconium came there; and having persuaded the multitudes, they stoned Paul and dragged him out of the city, supposing him to be dead. (Acts 14:19)

The very same people who were going to worship Paul one moment were persuaded to stone him to death the next!

After Paul was shipwrecked on the island of Malta, we find a story that is very similar in nature. The Scripture declares,

³But when Paul had gathered a bundle of sticks and laid them on the fire, a viper came out because of the heat, and fastened on his hand. ⁴So when the natives saw the creature hanging from his hand, they said to one another, "No doubt this man is a murderer, whom, though he has escaped the sea, yet justice does not allow to live." ⁵But he shook off the creature into the fire and suffered no harm. ⁶However, they were expecting that he would swell up or suddenly fall down dead. But after they had looked for a long time and saw no harm come to him, they changed their minds and said that he was a god. (Acts 28:3–6)

One minute they said he was a murderer, the next minute they said he was a god! It is wise to keep in mind how quickly people and their opinions can change!

Supposing Him to Be Dead

In Acts 14:19, we are told that the crowd had supposed that, after stoning him, Paul was dead. The reason the crowd thought he was dead was because he probably was (or so close to it that you couldn't tell the difference)! After he was stoned, they dragged his body out of the city and dumped it!

The stones they threw would have bruised him and torn his flesh. They likely crushed and broke bones and possibly caved in Paul's skull. Stoning was a form of execution. The purpose was to kill the victim. But when the disciples gathered around him something miraculous occurred. God raised him up!

²⁰However, when the disciples gathered around him, he rose up and went into the city. And the next day he departed with Barnabas to Derbe. ²¹And when they had preached the

> gospel to that city and made many disciples, they returned to Lystra, Iconium, and Antioch, [22]strengthening the souls of the disciples, exhorting them to continue in the faith, and saying, "We must through many tribulations enter the kingdom of God." (Acts 14:20–22)

We are not told if the disciples gathered around Paul's body to mourn him and take him away for burial or if they gathered around him to pray for a miracle. What we do know is that (either to their surprise or in answer to their prayer) God did raise Paul up and seemingly healed him so thoroughly that he made his way back into the city of Lystra for the night. The following morning, they made the twenty-mile journey to Derbe (an almost unimaginable journey for someone who had just been stoned and left for dead!).

As the stones were being hurled at him, did Paul think of Stephen, the Church's first martyr? Did he think of the part he had played in that murder? Did he remember the words of forgiveness that Stephen uttered with his dying breath?

We can only imagine, for we are not told. Was Paul raised up due to the earnest prayers of the disciples gathered around his lifeless body or was it a sovereign act of God? Again, we don't know because we are not told. What we do know is that our God still has the power to heal the sick and raise the dead and that the preaching of the gospel and making disciples should be our highest priority.

It was certainly the priority of Paul and Barnabas, for instead of quietly returning to their home church in Antioch of Syria, they went to the city of Derbe and continued to win souls and make disciples. After that, instead of heading to Tarsus and taking a ship directly and quickly to Seleucia and home, they made the long journey back to each city where they had won people to Christ in order to strengthen the souls of the new converts (and yes, they even returned to Lystra where Paul had been stoned, as well as to Antioch and Iconium, the cities their persecutors had followed them from!).

How precious is this gospel we have been commissioned and equipped to share! How valuable are the souls of men and women created in God's image! May we happily give our all and follow wherever He leads in order to win as many as we can, while we can, through any means we can!

Once Paul and Barnabas returned to their home church in Antioch, they faithfully reported all that God had done with them and that He had opened the door of faith to the Gentiles. Shortly thereafter, they did the same thing to the leaders of the Jerusalem church being careful to include a detailed report of all the miracles that God had wrought through them (Acts 14:26–27; 15:12).

CHAPTER
20

A Spirit of Divination and Unusual Miracles

Opposition

We were in a rented facility and there was just not enough room. It was the early days of Cottonwood Church. We were in a great season of momentum, and because of the crowds that were coming and the number of people who were turning to Christ, we had to keep adding services. Eventually we found a suitable piece of property on which we could build our own church. Once we decided to buy that piece of land and build, it seemed like all hell broke loose.

We had opposition from adjoining property owners, from people in a nearby neighborhood, and from certain city officials. One of the building contractors (who was not a Christian) even said, "I've never seen anything like this. Even my perfectly good equipment keeps breaking down. It's as if some unseen force doesn't want this church built!" He was right. The devil never gives up ground uncontested.

He will always oppose and try to thwart or hinder the work God is doing through His people.

In Acts 16, we find the story of how Paul and his team were supernaturally led to the Macedonian city of Philippi to preach the gospel. Right after they had won their first converts and baptized them, the opposition began. But it came in an interesting way . . .

> [16]Now it happened, as we went to prayer, that a certain slave girl possessed with a spirit of divination met us, who brought her masters much profit by fortune-telling. [17]This girl followed Paul and us, and cried out, saying, "These men are the servants of the Most High God, who proclaim to us the way of salvation." [18]And this she did for many days. But Paul, greatly annoyed, turned and said to the spirit, "I command you in the name of Jesus Christ to come out of her." And he came out that very hour. (Acts 16:16–18)

Everything this demon-possessed girl said was true, but who wants a demon advertising for them? Jesus had similar things happen and He always silenced the demons that were speaking, even though what those demons were saying was true (Mark 3:11–12).

Perhaps the girl who followed Paul and cried out day after day did so in a mocking or sarcastic voice. Whether that was the case or not, she certainly was causing people to associate the gospel message with the occult, as everyone in the area would have known who this girl was and what she did for her masters.

Paul, being greatly annoyed (inwardly grieved), finally cast the demon out of the girl. He was grieved and annoyed at the negative impact her announcements were having, but he was, no doubt, also grieved at the pitiful plight of the poor girl whose life was being ruled by a demon spirit and by heartless men.

It is true that this slave girl was not physically sick, and though physical healing is the main focus of this book, it is worth commenting on this story because in Scripture (as we have already discussed in previous chapters), evil spirits and disease are often connected. And whether it is a spirit of infirmity or a spirit of divination, as believers we are to deal with them the same way.

In Mark 16:17, Jesus said, "And these signs will follow those who believe: In My name they will cast out demons." That is exactly what the apostle Paul did. He turned and said to the spirit (not the girl), "I command you in the name of Jesus Christ to come out of her."

Ephesus

The apostle Paul tirelessly traveled, preaching the gospel in different regions, winning souls, and establishing churches. He experienced amazing favor and great opposition. In Acts 18, we find him preaching in a synagogue in Ephesus, that great city of the ancient world. He left Aquila and Priscilla there to carry on with the work while he traveled on.

Paul would, however, return to Ephesus where he would remain for several years, teaching, winning the lost to Christ, and helping the new converts grow in their relationship with the Lord. And in Ephesus, which was a great stronghold for witchcraft, idolatry, and the practice of magical arts, God would work unusual miracles through Paul, which in part led to a great move of the Holy Spirit in that city.

Unusual Miracles

> [8]And he went into the synagogue and spoke boldly for three months, reasoning and persuading concerning the things of the kingdom of God. [9]But when some were hardened and did not believe, but spoke evil of the Way before the

multitude, he departed from them and withdrew the disciples, reasoning daily in the school of Tyrannus. ¹⁰And this continued for two years, so that all who dwelt in Asia heard the word of the Lord Jesus, both Jews and Greeks. ¹¹Now God worked unusual miracles by the hands of Paul, ¹²so that even handkerchiefs or aprons were brought from his body to the sick, and the diseases left them and the evil spirits went out of them. (Acts 19:8–12)

When Paul returned to Ephesus, God worked unusual (extraordinary, in a special class) miracles by the hands of Paul. God worked the miracles; Paul was the vessel He used. These miracles brought healing to the sick and deliverance to those oppressed or possessed by demons. The word translated *handkerchiefs* in verse 11 literally refers to "a cloth used to wipe perspiration from one's brow." *Aprons* refers to "the work apron that Paul would have worn while plying his trade as a tent maker" (Acts 18:3; 20:34). God used some very natural things to work something very supernatural.

By referring to these miracles as *unusual*, we understand that they were not common. Healing the sick and setting demonic captives free are not unusual things when you consider the biblical record. It was the means that God used to work these miracles that made them unusual. We never see Paul being used this way again, and there is not a New Testament pattern of God using such means to bring healing elsewhere. That brings several thoughts to my mind that I would like to share with you here.

1. You cannot put God in a box.

We find from reading the New Testament that there are specific patterns that God has given us to follow in ministering to the sick. He has commanded all believers to lay hands on the sick for their recovery, and we are told that anointing the sick with oil and praying the prayer of faith will bring healing (Mark 16:17–18; James 5:14–15).

Yet we also find that on certain occasions God healed through touching the hem of a garment, spitting on someone's eyes, putting mud on someone's eyes and having them wash it off, dipping in a river seven times, laying a bunch of figs on a diseased area, being touched by a person's shadow, as well as several other means. We need to follow the pattern laid out for us in Scripture, yet be open for the Holy Spirit's leading to be used in an unusual way.

Sing Over Him

When our oldest son, Harrison, was a little boy, he came down with a terrible fever that resulted in him losing almost all of his hearing. We prayed and prayed, we laid hands on him, but there were no noticeable results. We took him to doctors, but there was nothing they could do to help him. He had lost about 80 percent of his hearing. It was heartbreaking as parents to talk to our son and get no response from him unless we were facing him and he could see that we were speaking, and even then, we had to raise our voices to an uncomfortable level in order for him to hear.

One night as I was praying and talking to God about the situation, the Holy Spirit said to me, *"Go and sing over him."* I went into Harrison's bedroom and stood over him as he slept. I lifted my hands and began to worship God in song. It was hard at first. I didn't feel like singing or worshiping at all. My heart was breaking for my son. Five minutes, ten minutes, fifteen minutes, I continued to sing.

At about twenty minutes, something happened. A note of joy and victory came into my spirit. The heaviness I was feeling was gone and was replaced by a real sense of God's presence. I sang for a couple more minutes and went to bed. In the morning, when our son woke up, his hearing was restored! God had healed him.

A Slap in the Face

Before I was married, I served as an assistant pastor in a small church. As part of my duties, twice a month I would go to a neighboring town and hold meetings in a local community center. On one of those evenings, after I had finished preaching, I asked that people in need of healing come forward for prayer. Several people began to get out of their seats and walk to the front.

One of those people was a woman I had never seen in our meetings before. As she walked closer to where I was standing, in my spirit, I saw myself doing something. It is hard to explain, but I knew the Holy Spirit was telling me to act. It all happened so fast that I almost did it without thinking. When she got close enough, I slapped her in the face! That's right. I slapped this woman (whom I had never met) in the face in front of everyone!

She was stunned and so was I. I thought to myself, *Did I really just do that?* Then, looking me in the eye, she asked, "Can I have the microphone?" I handed her the microphone, having no idea what was coming next. She looked at the crowd, who all seemed to be in a state of shock over what I had done, and said, "This man is of God. Several years ago, a man struck me in the face and I lost all feeling in that side of my face as a result. But when this man struck me, all of my feeling just returned. I am healed!" Boy, was I grateful! I went from thinking, *O God, what did I just do*, to thinking, *O God, You are amazing!*

I would put both singing over my son and slapping the lady in the category of *unusual*. I don't think that I have ever sung over a sick person again and I know that I've never slapped anyone again!

2. Don't try and turn the exception into the rule.

As obvious as this point is, it does need to be stated. God, at times and by the leading of the Spirit, may have us do some unusual things. But we must remember that they are just that—unusual, extraordinary, and not a part of the established pattern.

Yet, I have known (and you probably have too) of men and women who have built things like this into the core of what they do in their ministries. They offer trinkets or cloths or little vials of special water to their listeners in exchange for a donation to their work, claiming that the item has a special healing anointing stored in it.

It is unfortunate that such things go on. And please don't get me wrong: I think it is fine for ministries to send some kind of gift as a sign of appreciation to those who faithfully support the work they do, but some have gone far beyond that and trespassed into an area outside of the bounds of Scripture. And again, sometimes God may use unusual means to do His work, but let us be careful not to try and turn the exception into the rule.

The Word Grew Mightily and Prevailed

As the story of the gospel's impact in Ephesus continues to unfold, we find that a group of Jewish exorcists tried to cast out a demon "by the Jesus whom Paul preaches" (Acts 19:13). Their failure and the subsequent trouncing of all seven of them by the demon-possessed man became known to everyone in the city.

God used all of these events to arrest the people's attention and to magnify the name of Jesus. A great multitude was swept into the kingdom as a result. And when they turned their lives over to Jesus, they made a clean break with their past occult practices. It truly is an amazing story. In summing up what was happening in Ephesus, the

Scriptures say, "So the word of the Lord grew mightily and prevailed" (Acts 19:20).

That is important. For if we look closely at the whole story, we find that upon his first visit to Ephesus Paul preached the Word in a synagogue there. When he departed, he left Aquila and Priscilla to continue teaching. Apollos also taught the Word in Ephesus. Once Paul returned, he spent three years daily teaching God's Word in a synagogue, in the Greek philosophy school of Tyrannus, publicly, and from house to house (Acts 18:18–21, 24–26; 19:8–10; 20:17–21, 26–31).

Three years of continually sowing the incorruptible seed of God's Word! We cannot separate that from the miracles and healings that occurred or from the radical salvations that took place. God tallied it all up by saying, "***So the word of the Lord grew mightily and prevailed.***"

G. Campbell Morgan says that means "it grew with resistless and overpowering strength."[1] It grew and prevailed over demons, disease, superstition, the occult, and ultimately over the devil's grip on the people of Ephesus.

Dear friend, the Word of the Lord has not lost any of its prevailing power. Read it. Meditate upon it. Share it. It will produce all of the results that we saw it produce in the ancient city of Ephesus if we stay with it and give it the priority that the apostle Paul gave it in his day. Job put it well when he said, "I have not departed from the commandments of His lips; I have treasured the words of His mouth more than my necessary food" (Job 23:12).

CHAPTER

21

Dead Men, Shipwrecks, and Snake Bites

A Case for Common Sense

⁷Now on the first day of the week, when the disciples came together to break bread, Paul, ready to depart the next day, spoke to them and continued his message until midnight. ⁸There were many lamps in the upper room where they were gathered together. ⁹And in a window sat a certain young man named Eutychus, who was sinking into a deep sleep. He was overcome by sleep; and as Paul continued speaking, he fell down from the third story and was taken up dead. ¹⁰But Paul went down, fell on him, and embracing him said, "Do not trouble yourselves, for his life is in him." ¹¹Now when he had come up, had broken bread and eaten, and talked a long while, even till daybreak, he departed. ¹²And they brought the young man in alive, and they were not a little comforted. (Acts 20:7–12)

Paul, along with his team, was spending a week in the city of Troas. It was the night before their departure that the events in this story occurred. The believers in that area had gathered in an upper room to listen to Paul's farewell message. And it was a long one.

Robertson, a Bible commentator, sagely noted, "Preachers usually have some excuse for the long sermon which is not always clear to the exhausted audience."[1]

I have suffered myself, numerous times, under a long-winded preacher who didn't have much to say (and I must admit that I have gone far too long in my preaching a few times myself). In this case, however, I don't think we can accuse Paul of exhausting his audience. He was leaving Troas in the morning, they were new converts to Christ, and he had much important information to give them. Their ability to thrive spiritually in a hostile environment may have very well depended on the things he was teaching them. They were eager listeners.

Yet even though his message was of utmost importance and they were eager to hear it, we must remember that we still have this treasure in earthen vessels that become weary and need sleep. Such was the case of a young man named Eutychus. He was battling to stay awake and listen, but eventually, no doubt because of the stuffiness of the room, the smoke from the burning lamps, and the lateness of the hour, he lost the battle and was overcome by sleep.

In that upper room they had the natural illumination from the lamps and the spiritual light that comes from hearing the Word (Psalm 119:130), *but they seemed to be lacking the light of common sense.*

The window that Eutychus was sitting in would not have been glazed. It probably had latticework, but that would have been open due to the crowd and the many lamps that were burning in that upper room.

It was an unwise place to be sitting, as it was a straight drop, three stories to the ground.

We, like all good parents, have watched out for our children and warned them to avoid dangerous places. Apparently, no one thought to warn Eutychus. Even as he was trying to stay awake, he should have realized that sitting on that windowsill was a dangerous place to be if he should fall asleep. Better to take a seat on the floor than to flirt with something so precarious.

Under the Mower

I have a friend who had a huge front yard. It was so large he had to use a sit-down power mower to get the job done in a reasonable time. One day as he was out mowing, his little boy began to race back and forth in front of the mower. My friend did not stop him, after all, it seemed extremely unlikely that anything could happen.

But it did. While streaking by, his boy tripped and fell towards the oncoming mower. By the time my friend was able to stop it, his son's foot had already gone underneath. It cut his foot to the bone. By the grace of God, he didn't lose his foot. After surgery and a short time of rehab, he was able to walk and run again normally. The moral of the story is that *it never should have happened*! It was the result of the failure to exercise a little common sense.

All of us can think of times when difficulties could have been utterly avoided had we or the people we know used some common sense. And as crazy as it sounds, it is quite common for people who fail to use common sense to blame the results of their lack of proper judgment on God (my friend, by the way, did not blame God for what had happened to his boy). Solomon put it well when he said, "People ruin their lives with the foolish things they do, and then they blame the Lord for it" (Proverbs 19:3 ERV).

Fortunate

The young man who fell to his death was named Eutychus, which means "fortunate." It was unfortunate that he fell asleep and plummeted to the ground below while the preacher was giving his message, but he was fortunate that the preacher was Paul. When King Ahaziah fell through the lattice of his upper room, he sought the help of a pagan god (2 Kings 1:2) and he died. Eutychus, who fell three stories to his death, had Paul to intercede on his behalf. Paul knew the right place to go for help. He looked to the living God, who raised Eutychus up.

Dr. Luke leaves no doubt about the young man's state after his fall. He tells us in certain terms that he was taken up, or picked up, *dead*. When Paul went down to the street, he fell on him and embraced him, suddenly announcing, "His life is in him." Paul's act was reminiscent of what Elijah did with the dead body of the widow's son or Elisha with the body of the Shunamite's son (1 Kings 17:21–22; 2 Kings 4:34). Perhaps Paul was thinking of these very stories as he embraced the lifeless body of Eutychus.

Desire the Gifts

One thing is certain. It takes something beyond ordinary faith to raise the dead. It is only through the operation of the gifts of the Spirit that the dead are raised. When something so spectacular takes place, it is generally the result of the gift of special faith, the working of miracles, and the gifts of healings in operation (1 Corinthians 12:7–11). If a person who is raised up is not healed of the disease or injuries that caused their death, they would just die again right away.

Many years ago, when I was serving as an assistant pastor, I was preaching one evening from 1 Corinthians on the gifts of the Spirit. As I was speaking, I was suddenly seized with an urgency to emphasize that we are told to desire spiritual gifts (1 Corinthians 12:31; 14:1, 39).

I actually began to say over and over, "*You have to desire the gifts!*" I probably said it five or six times. A few days later I knew why God had me emphasize that point.

It was a couple of days later that the senior pastor of our church, along with his family, were enjoying a dinner at the home of some friends. After the meal, the kids all went upstairs to play while the adults cleared the table and washed the dishes. Once upstairs, the older children climbed through a window out onto the roof.

The 3-year-old son of the senior pastor decided to follow them. He lost his balance and fell from the roof to the ground two stories below. The pastor's wife was washing dishes when she saw through the kitchen window, which opened into the back yard, what looked like a rag being thrown down (that is how she described it).

When the children on the roof began to shout, everyone realized that it was no rag that had hit the ground, but one of the children. I will never forget when the pastor told me the story. He said, "I ran outside, only to see the lifeless body of my son on the ground. One of his arms was bent at an unnatural angle underneath him. I scooped him up in my arms. He was not moving and there seemed to be no life in him."

That's when he said he suddenly heard my voice saying, "You've got to desire the gifts! Desire the gifts!" He began to pray like he'd never prayed before. "'I desire the gifts! God, I desire the gifts!' Suddenly, something that felt like warm electricity hit me in the top of the head," he said. "It traveled down to my feet and then came back up and flowed out my arms into my son's body. He opened his eyes and said, 'Hi, dad!' Then he jumped out of my arms and ran off to play with the other kids!"

What a blessing to know that we serve the Lord, who does not change. He is still working wonders in the midst of His people today.

Unlike the pastor's son, who rejoined the other children to play, it seems that Eutychus did not rejoin the meeting. Maybe he went and got some of that sleep he was so desperately in need of! After returning to the upper room, Paul and the others broke bread and began to talk, which continued until daybreak. In the morning, Eutychus joined them again, which greatly comforted everyone present.

Hopefully Eutychus remembered throughout his life how the Lord had mercy on him and raised him up. Janet and I have always tried to make it our practice, as parents, to remind and rehearse to our children about the times God answered our prayers and healed them when they were small.

We never want to forget His acts of grace and mercy and we want our children to think of them often. It never pays to have a short memory when it comes to the goodness and intervention of God that we have experienced in our lives (Psalm 77:11–12; 78:41–42; Matthew 16:9–10).

Shipwrecked on an Island

Acts 27 records the riveting story of a portion of Paul's journey as a prisoner to Rome. After boarding a second ship, Paul perceived (no doubt, by the Spirit) that the voyage would end with disaster and much loss.

Even though Paul advised everyone of this, the Roman centurion in charge of him put more stock in the opinions of the helmsman, the owner of the ship, and the majority than in what Paul said, and promptly put Paul and his companions aboard. Between Paul, his companions, the other passengers, the Roman soldiers, and the sailors, there was a total of 276 people on board. It would be a voyage they never would forget.

As they progressed, they were caught in a terrible storm, which was so bad and lasted for so long that eventually everyone gave up all hope of survival. At their darkest hour, Paul rekindled the fires of hope in their hearts as he told them about an angelic appearance and the promise given to him by God that they would all be saved.

"However," he told them, "we must run aground on a certain island" (Acts 27:26). And it happened just that way. The ship was lost, but everyone made it safely to land. Whether Paul knew it or not, that storm had brought them to the doorstep of a people in need. And now, more than thirty years after Peter preached that first sermon on the day of Pentecost, we find the Lord is still stretching out His hands to heal.

> [1]Now when they had escaped, they then found out that the island was called Malta. [2]And the natives showed us unusual kindness; for they kindled a fire and made us all welcome, because of the rain that was falling and because of the cold. [3]But when Paul had gathered a bundle of sticks and laid them on the fire, a viper came out because of the heat, and fastened on his hand. [4]So when the natives saw the creature hanging from his hand, they said to one another, "No doubt this man is a murderer, whom, though he has escaped the sea, yet justice does not allow to live." [5]But he shook off the creature into the fire and suffered no harm. [6]However, they were expecting that he would swell up or suddenly fall down dead. But after they had looked for a long time and saw no harm come to him, they changed their minds and said that he was a god. (Acts 28:1–6)

I Deserved to Be Bitten

When I was a kid, my dad and I used to hike into some local mountains to fly fish for trout. Once we got to the area we wanted to fish, he would go upstream and I would go downstream. Eventually, we would meet back at a designated spot to cook and eat the trout we had caught.

On one of these trips, as I made my way downstream I caught a small garter snake. For a little boy, that makes a day of fishing all the better. I played with him for a while and then put him in my creel with the trout I had caught. After about half an hour, I took him out and played with him a little more.

That process was repeated three or four times until I'm sure that little snake had had enough. The next time I took him out of my creel, he wasted no time in biting me. He was small, but his bite still hurt. I had two bright red fang marks on the back of my hand where he had gotten me. I promptly dropped him and off he went. The truth is I deserved to be bitten by that poor snake! I'm sure he thought of what I had perceived as fun as torment!

Being bitten on the hand by a snake is something I have in common with the apostle Paul. However, the snake that bit me was harmless while the snake that bit him was quite venomous. Also, while I deserved the bite I received, Paul did not. In fact, after his ordeal of being lost at sea, shipwrecked, rained on, and being exposed to the bitter cold, he busied himself gathering wood for the fire! He was bitten while engaged in a good work.

Some Thoughts and Observations About Paul's Encounter with the Viper

1. Start a fire and the serpent will show up.

There is a powerful metaphor that can be drawn from this story. Paul told Timothy, "I would remind you to stir up (rekindle the embers of, fan the flame of, and keep burning) the [gracious] gift of God, [the inner fire] that is in you" (2 Timothy 1:6 AMPC).

The two men on the road to Emmaus said, "Did not our heart burn within us while He talked with us on the road, and while He opened the Scriptures to us?" (Luke 24:32). The point is that whenever you get a fire going in your life for God, whenever the things of God begin to burn brightly in your soul, you can expect the serpent to show up.

Whether it is a fresh consecration to prayer, to studying the Scriptures, to sharing the good news, or to giving obediently and sacrificially to support kingdom work, the serpent will try and get you to back off. He will sink his fangs into your body, your marriage, your children, or your business. He will bring pressure and persecution, all with the purpose of getting you to back up or cool off in your commitment.

Anyone who has walked with God for any length of time will know this by experience. The question is *how should we respond to these attacks by the serpent*. The answer is *the same way Paul did . . . shake it off*! We must rise up and use the authority we have in Jesus' name.

Jesus said, "Behold, I give you the authority to trample on serpents and scorpions, and over all the power of the enemy, and nothing shall by any means hurt you" (Luke 10:19). James tells us that once we have submitted ourselves to God we should resist the devil and he will flee from us (James 4:7).

As children of the Most High, we can shake off oppression! We can shake off fear and every other work of the enemy! For some reading this now, it is high time for you to put your foot down and say, "*Enough! Devil, you can't have my health, my marriage, my children, or my business! I resist you in Jesus' name!*" Shake him off!

2. Don't tempt God.

The serpent that bit Paul in this account was not metaphorical by any means. It was a real serpent with a lethal bite. In fact, once again, Dr. Luke uses medical terms to describe what should have happened to Paul once he was bitten. The phrase "swell up" found in verse 6 was a common medical term meaning to become inflamed and cause swelling.

But Paul didn't stick his hand out so the serpent could bite him. He wasn't handling the serpent as some kind of proof that he had faith. That would have been tempting the Lord. Jesus would not throw Himself from the temple even though there was a scriptural promise of angels bearing us up in their hands. He said to do so would be to tempt the Lord our God (Luke 4:9–12). Paul being bitten by the serpent was completely unexpected and unplanned. If things like that happen, like him, we can trust God to keep us well.

Sharks in the Lagoon

A group of people that I know went on a short-term mission trip to a developing country. Upon their arrival, the local minister hosting the trip told them that they shouldn't drink any water except the bottled water that he had provided. He went on to tell them that the regional tap water was filled with bacteria and would make them sick.

Some of those in the group arrogantly said, "This local water won't harm us. God will protect us." Their host went on to tell them of a local lagoon that was filled with sharks. "Would you go swimming in the lagoon? It's safer than drinking the water," he said. "Just because you can't see the bacteria like you can the sharks, that doesn't make it less dangerous."

Some of those in the group still insisted that they could drink the water with no ill effects. It would have been one thing if the contaminated water was all they had to drink, but they had an ample supply of bottled water at their disposal.

So, against their host's admonition, a portion of the team went ahead and drank freely from the local tap water "by faith." Those that did so all got violently ill and were not of much use for the rest of the trip. What was the issue? It was one of presumption and pride disguised as an act of faith.

3. God has not brought you this far to abandon you now.

God had delivered Paul repeatedly and sustained him through many dangerous situations. There had been multiple attempts on his life. He had been forced to appeal to Caesar because of the plotting of the Jews. He was forced aboard a ship as a prisoner. He went through a terrible storm at sea and was shipwrecked on an island. He was tired and wet and cold, and then he gets bitten by a snake! By this point, many of us would be thinking, *Really? A snake?! I didn't think much else could go wrong!*

The truth was God had not brought Paul through so much difficulty to abandon him at this point. And God has not brought you this far to abandon you! You may have just exited one storm to find yourself entering into another, or just when it seemed like nothing else could go wrong, you got bitten by a serpent.

Listen carefully. Neither your storm nor your snake bites have taken God by surprise. He has His eye on you. He is with you and He will help you. Scripture tells us, "For He Himself has said, 'I will never leave you nor forsake you.' So we may boldly say: 'The Lord is my helper; I will not fear. What can man do to me?'" (Hebrews 13:5–6). Trust Him.

4. The crowd is fickle.

Here, the crowd went from thinking Paul was a murderer to thinking he was a god, while in Lystra the crowd went from calling him a god to murdering him (Acts 14:8–19). The crowd is always fickle. People sometimes shift very quickly in their opinions and many are easily carried away by whatever someone is shouting, taking it as the truth. The result is that those who are magnified one moment may be vilified the next.

There are several lessons that we can immediately take away from this. First, we must never let the crowd be the determining factor in what we believe or how we act. It is true that many people prefer to let others think for them, so whatever the popular consensus of the crowd is at the moment, that is what they embrace.

Such people are either too lazy or too afraid to come up with and stand by their own conclusions, so they always default to the most popular opinions of the time. Critical thinkers are rare, and even rarer are those who dare to defy the crowd and move in a different direction than it is going.

The second lesson that is immediately clear (at least to me) is that we should not be moved by the crowd when they are for us or when they are against us. At the end of the day we must give an account to the One who called us. We must give our all in performing His will. It is the truth of His Word that must be our final authority in all matters of belief, conduct, and living, whether or not it is popular and accepted by the crowd or by modern culture. If we allow the fear of man to shape and mold our speech and actions, we cannot be the servants of Christ (Galatians 1:10; Proverbs 29:25; Psalm 119:128; Romans 3:4).

5. Difficulties are not a sign of displeasure.

When the island locals saw the viper bite Paul, they immediately assumed and said that it was some form of divine punishment. If difficulties were a sign of God's displeasure, then the apostle Paul was almost never the recipient of God's smile or favor. His life, by his own admission, was continually fraught with danger and difficulties (2 Corinthians 11:23–33).

More than anything else, Paul's difficulties and distresses were a sign that he was on the right track. They were spawned by the enemy who will do all he can to thwart the forward progress of the kingdom (Ephesians 6:10–20). It has been aptly said that if you are taking flack, you are over the right target.

Robertson put it well when he noted, "These people thought that calamity was proof of guilt, poor philosophy and worse theology."[2]

Unfortunately, some people in the Church are far too quick to render judgment (even if it is whispered in gossip) concerning their brothers and sisters who are going through a rough patch or facing a dilemma. If you have brought trouble on yourself through unwise or sinful choices, repent and look to God for help. He is merciful and ready to aid His children in need.

And if you know that your present struggle is the direct result of the enemy's work, resist him in the name of Jesus, carry on in obedience to God, and pay no attention to the self-appointed judges and critics who would condemn you.

Hospitality and Healing

As the story of their shipwreck progressed, we find an account of both hospitality and healing. The chief official of the island hospitably welcomed Paul and the others, not realizing what a blessing it would be for his household as well as for the other inhabitants of the island.

> ⁷In that region there was an estate of the leading citizen of the island, whose name was Publius, who received us and entertained us courteously for three days. ⁸And it happened that the father of Publius lay sick of a fever and dysentery. Paul went in to him and prayed, and he laid his hands on him and healed him. ⁹So when this was done, the rest of those on the island who had diseases also came and were healed. ¹⁰They also honored us in many ways; and when we departed, they provided such things as were necessary. ¹¹After three months we sailed in an Alexandrian ship whose figurehead was the Twin Brothers, which had wintered at the island. (Acts 28:7–11)

Luke uses very specific medical terms when describing the condition of the father of Publius. *Dysentery* refers to "an infection of the intestines marked by severe diarrhea." It was often accompanied with severe abdominal pain and dehydration and often proved fatal. The word he uses for "fever" is actually plural, meaning "fevers." It was a term used by doctors in the ancient world to describe intermittent fevers, or fevers that would come and go. The father of Publius was in a bad way, and by looking at the medical terms Luke used in describing him, we could safely say that his life was in jeopardy.

Although Dr. Luke uses natural medical terms to describe the case of the father of Publius, he explicitly tells us that the cure was supernatural in nature. Paul prayed and laid his hands on him, which brought about his healing. After this happened, all of the other sick people on the island also came and were healed, no doubt, by the same means.

Paul and the other survivors of the shipwreck stayed on Malta for three months. During that time, a steady stream (so it is inferred by the Greek) of sick people came to Paul and were healed. What the enemy meant for evil, God, by His grace and power, turned into an island-wide healing meeting where the name of Jesus was magnified.

Some Thoughts and Observations About the Healings That Occurred on Malta

1. An atmosphere conducive to healing

Publius was the leading citizen of the island. That literally means that he was the Roman governor of the island. He was kind, courteous, and generous. It seems that the spirit of kindness and hospitality that the islanders showed started at the top. That is generally true of a village, a church, or an organization.

Rude and Delightful

Some time ago, my wife and I had the opportunity to interact with a number of people who all belonged to the same company. They were serving their organization at different levels of leadership, but they all had one thing in common . . . they were rude!

From the front-line person on the lowest level to the high-tiered executive, every one of them was rude and unpleasant. A short time later we had the same basic interactions with the employees of a different company in the same industry. From top to bottom they had something in common as well . . . they were all delightful!

They were helpful and it was a pleasure to be around every one of them. Good or bad, it usually comes from the top down.

I share this for a reason. I believe that the openness, kindness, and hospitality of those living on Malta helped create an atmosphere conducive to healing. If they had been hostile or resentful from the start toward those who had been shipwrecked, or if Publius hadn't *received* them (v. 7), it is doubtful that his father would have *received* his healing. The natives of the island showed them *unusual* kindness (v. 2), not knowing that the one they were entertaining had been used by God to perform *unusual* miracles of healing (Acts 19:11).

An inescapable truth is that you cannot have a closed heart toward people and have an open heart toward God at the same time.

2. The command to lay hands on the sick for healing has never been rescinded.

Jesus laid His hands on the sick and healed them. The apostles did the same. Before His ascension, Jesus commanded all believers to lay hands on the sick to bring healing to them. It is a command that has never been rescinded.

Here on the island of Malta, some thirty-plus years after Jesus ascended into heaven, Paul is doing what the Lord commanded all believers to do. The results were spectacular, indeed, but they were the Lord's doing as He worked in partnership with one of His obedient children.

If you are a believer and you have hands, you are responsible for doing this. When we lay our hands on the sick in obedient faith to Christ's command, we become His conduits to bring healing to those in need. He is the one who heals—that is His responsibility. Our part is to obey His command (Luke 4:40; Acts 5:12; Mark 16:17–18).

3. The dinner bell

An acquaintance told me about his life on a ranch when he was a boy. There were lots of employees and family members working at various jobs throughout the day on the property. Some were mending fences, others were working with cattle, some were doing chores in the barn while others worked on various projects with machinery, land cultivation, and so on.

"But," he said, "whenever the cook rang the dinner bell, everyone stopped what they were doing and came back to the main building to eat." He went on to tell me, "Divine healing is the dinner bell! It will bring people from far and wide because there is always a need for healing."

That has always stuck with me. We see it here on the island of Malta. Once the father of Publius was healed, *everyone else* on the island who was sick came for healing as well. How did they find out about the father of Publius? Good news travels fast. People talked about it. It was the dinner bell to bring them in so they could be introduced to a merciful Savior who could heal sick bodies and forgive sins (Luke 5:20–24).

Every Sunday Night

Every Sunday night in our church for over twenty-two years, I taught on divine healing and we prayed for the sick. Throughout that time we witnessed the Lord healing people from almost every sickness imaginable. We saw people healed of cancer, paralysis, deafness, and many other things. One thing that constantly occurred in conjunction with the healings that took place was that new people came.

Family members, friends, and co-workers of those who were healed would come. Sometimes they came because they were curious. Sometimes because God had used the miracle to convict their heart. And sometimes because they needed healing themselves.

One of the things that invariably happened is that people got saved. Almost every Sunday night, without fail, people came to Christ. The dinner bell brought them in and when we shared the plan of salvation, many put their faith in Jesus.

4. God didn't cause the storm, but He certainly used it.

Nothing takes God by surprise. God may not have caused the storm, but He wove it into His plans to reach the people of Malta (see chapter 7 under "No Accident").

You may be in the middle of one of life's storms right now. Circumstances may be threatening to ruin you. Take heart because He is still mightier than the storm. As the psalmist of old said, "The Lord on high is mightier than the noise of many waters, than the mighty waves of the sea" (Psalm 93:4).

Even as the storm brought Paul to an island full of people in need of healing and salvation, your storm may be bringing you to one of the greatest ministry opportunities of your life. Be open for God to direct you and use you.

The Church Grew While I Was Away

For quite a few years, my wife and I worked very proactively to reach, raise up, and release a large number of young people to carry on the work of Cottonwood Church (the church we founded in 1983). We had a number of young, anointed, and faithful men and women serving in various capacities in the ministry, and then it happened.

I was in a near fatal boating accident. I was not expected to live, but I did. Even after I became stable, due to the fact that there had been such severe damage to my throat in the accident, it was unknown whether I would ever be able to preach again. I was in the hospital for a long time, after which I convalesced at home. All in all, I was out of the pulpit and away from my duties in the church for six months.

When I came back, I was in for a surprise. The church had grown while I was away. It had grown in heart, influence, finances, and numbers while I was gone. All of the young people we had been training (and others) had to step up to the plate and assume leadership roles and responsibilities that were beyond what they had previously carried. I was pleasantly stunned.

It didn't take me long to realize that God had used the accident and my absence to bring the church to a new level. I clearly understood that I would have been far too slow in releasing some of the key younger leaders into their present roles.

It was obvious to me that it would have been a step backward for me to assume all of my former duties, so we adjusted. My wife and I are still very involved in church life and I still preach fairly often, but I am no longer doing the day-to-day or casting the vision for the future. Both my roles and my wife's have changed somewhat in this new season, but we are still busy for the Lord and loving life.

The storm and subsequent shipwreck were no doubt miserable things to go through, but God used them. Some of those on board may have cursed their luck for having to go through such things, but there were plenty on the island of Malta that would have felt very lucky and thankful to God for what that storm brought to their shores.

5. A witness for the risen Christ

Though there is no record that the apostle Paul preached the gospel to the inhabitants of Malta, I think we can safely assume that the one who said, "Woe is me if I do not preach the gospel!" would have spoken to the islanders about the Savior (1 Corinthians 9:16).

All of the supernatural healings that occurred were, in themselves, an irrefutable witness of the risen Christ. Dead people don't heal anyone.

Interestingly enough, we have received correspondence from people living on Malta today who watch our gospel broadcast. Who knows, they may even be the descendants of those that God used Paul to reach in his day.

6. They honored, but they did not pay.

After all the people came and were healed, Luke said, "They also honored us in many ways; and when we departed, they provided such things as were necessary" (Acts 28:10). They honored Paul and the others by providing everything necessary for their onward journey, but it was not given as a payment for their healings. The gifts of God cannot be purchased with money (Acts 8:20).

Giving to support a particular ministry's work out of gratitude or honor for what they have done or how they have helped you or someone that you love is a good thing, but it should never be looked at as some kind of payment for God's mercy.

It is unsafe ground when the minister expects or requires a reward from people for his services, even in an indirect way, or if the recipient of the blessings that flow through that ministry looks at any gift they give as some sort of payment. When Naaman tried to pay for his healing, Elisha refused to receive it (2 Kings 5:15–16).

The previous hospitality and kindness of those on Malta did not pay for their healing, and their gifts afterward did not pay for their healing. Their prior openness and kindness helped create an atmosphere conducive to healing, and the gifts they gave afterward were just an expression of thanksgiving and further kindness from the same people.

Jesus said to His disciples, "And as you go, preach, saying, 'The kingdom of heaven is at hand.' **Heal the sick, cleanse the lepers, raise** *the dead, cast out demons. Freely you have received, freely give"* (Matthew 10:7–8, emphasis mine).

The gospel is free. Healing is free. It has been paid for already through Christ's sacrifice on the cross. Having said that, however, it still is a scriptural principle to honor the Lord with the first part of all our income and to support His work consistently and generously with our finances.

And personally, I find it hard to fathom a stingy Christian. We serve the most generous and gracious God, and as His children, we should become more and more like Him every day (Proverbs 3:9; Malachi 3:10; 2 Corinthians 9:6–8; 1 Corinthians 9:7–14).

After setting sail from Malta, they eventually reached Rome where Paul continued to preach the gospel about a living Savior who forgives, heals, baptizes in the Holy Spirit, and is coming again.

Conclusion

Well, you've done it. You have read this book (or at least parts of it). Healing is available to you if you need it. We serve the Lord who does not change. He is still the same merciful Healer today as we read about in Luke and Acts. Look to Him. Trust His Word. And make yourself available to Him to be used as His vessel to bring healing to others.

NOTES

Chapter 1

1. G. Campbell Morgan, *The Gospel According to Luke* (Wipf & Stock, 1931), 69.
2. Morgan, *The Gospel According to Luke*, 69.
3. Morgan, *The Gospel According to Luke*, 63.

Chapter 9

1. Archibald Thomas Robertson, *The Gospel According to Luke,* Vol. II of *Word Pictures in the New Testament* (Baker Book House, 1930), 134.

Chapter 10

1. B.W. Johnson, *The Four Gospels and Acts of the Apostles,* Vol. I of *The People's New Testament* (Christian Publishing Company, 1889), 278.
2. G. Campbell Morgan, *The Gospel According to Luke* (Wipf & Stock, 1931), 168.

Chapter 11

1. Charles Caldwell Ryrie, *The Ryrie Study Bible: New Testament* (The Moody Bible Institute of Chicago, 1976), 402.

Chapter 14

1. G. Campbell Morgan, *The Acts of the Apostles* (Fleming H. Revell Company, 1924), 97.

Chapter 15

1. G. Campbell Morgan, *The Acts of the Apostles* (Fleming H. Revell Company, 1924), 133.

Chapter 19

1. Herbert Lockyer, *All the Miracles of the Bible* (Zondervan Publishing House, 1961), 282.

Chapter 20

1. G. Campbell Morgan, *The Acts of the Apostles* (Fleming H. Revell Company, 1924), 456.

Chapter 21

1. Archibald Thomas Robertson, *The Acts of the Apostles,* Vol. III of *Word Pictures in the New Testament* (Baker Book House, 1930), 340.
2. Robertson, *The Acts of the Apostles,* 479.

A Quick Reference for Your Thoughts and Questions

Examples of how to pray for healing.
- p. 32–33
- p. 109–115
- p. 168–176
- p. 187–191
- p. 234–237
- p. 256–259
- p. 276

If you are fearful.
- p. 103–107

If you have a loved one who is sick.
- p. 41–44
- p. 97–100

How can I be sure that healing is God's will for me?
- p. 22–25
- p. 31–33
- p. 179–182

If healing is for all, why are not all healed?
- p. 15–21
- p. 46–47
- p. 230–236

Quick Reference

I was prayed for but nothing happened.
- p. 120–124

Is sickness ever caused by an evil spirit?
- p. 93–95
- p. 125–134

Why do bad things sometimes happen to good people?
- p. 230–236

What role does faith have when it comes to healing?
- p. 35–39
- p. 57–58
- p. 63–72
- p. 80–82
- p. 121–124
- p. 142–146
- p. 147–149
- p. 151–155
- p. 207–211
- p. 242–244

The proper response when you or someone you know is healed.
- p. 22–24
- p. 83–87
- p. 91–93
- p. 149

www.ingramcontent.com/pod-product-compliance
Lightning Source LLC
Chambersburg PA
CBHW020242010526
44107CB00039B/1466/J